TEACH
WHAT YOU
BELIEVE

Also by Deacon Michael E. Bulson
Published by Paulist Press

PREACH WHAT YOU BELIEVE: Timeless Homilies for Deacons, Liturgical Cycle B

BELIEVE WHAT YOU READ: Timeless Homilies for Deacons, Liturgical Cycle C

TEACH WHAT YOU BELIEVE

Timeless Homilies for Deacons

LITURGICAL CYCLE A

Deacon Michael E. Bulson

PAULIST PRESS
New York/Mahwah, NJ

Cover design by Cynthia Dunne
Book design by Lynn Else

Cover art: Icon of Saint Philip the Deacon, Christ the Saviour Cathedral, Moscow, photograph by David Lucs, Orthodox Church in America, www.oca.org. Used by permission

Library of Congress Cataloging-in-Publication Data

Bulson, Michael E.
    Teach what you believe : timeless homilies for deacons : liturgical cycle A / Michael E. Bulson.
       p. cm.
    Includes bibliographical references.
    ISBN-13: 978-0-8091-4481-5 (alk. paper)
    1. Church year sermons. 2. Catholic Church—Sermons. 3. Sermons, American—21st century. 4. Catholic Church. Lectionary for Mass (U.S.).
    Year A. I. Title.
    BX1756.B827T43 2007
    252′.02—dc22

                                    2007010214

Published by Paulist Press
997 Macarthur Boulevard
Mahwah, New Jersey 07430

www.paulistpress.com

Printed and bound in the United States of America

CONTENTS

ACKNOWLEDGMENTS

"The Moon Cannot Be Stolen," from *Zen Flesh, Zen Bones* by Paul Reps, copyright © 1989 by Paul Reps and Charles E. Tuttle Co., Inc., of Boston, Massachusetts, and Tokyo, Japan. Reprinted by permission of Tuttle Publishing Co., Inc.

"A Hole in a Flute," from *The Gift* by Daniel Ladinsky, copyright © 1999 by Daniel Ladinsky. Reprinted by permission of the author.

"The Mercy of God" from *The Selected Poetry of Jessica Powers* published by ICS Publications, Washington, D.C. © 1999 Carmelite Monastery, Pewaukee, WI. Used with permission.

Excerpt from "Ash Wednesday" in *Collected Poems 1909-1962* by T.S. Eliot, copyright © 1963 by T.S. Eliot and renewed in 1968, 1969, 1971, 1972, 1982, 1984, 1991 by Esme Valerie Eliot, reprinted by permission of Harcourt, Inc., and Faber and Faber, Ltd.

DEDICATION

To the people of St. Joseph Catholic Parish, Ogden, Utah,
with gratitude for their generosity and goodness.

APPRECIATIONS

I continue to be grateful for the support of my wife, Mary Lou, for her patience and expertise, especially with reading and correcting the text. Thank you also to Marcy and John Thaeler for their ongoing support and encouragement. And I continue to be indebted to my editor at Paulist, Kevin Carrizo di Camillo, for his skillful and gracious help on this book as well as those that preceded it.

INTRODUCTION

In August 2000, a few years after I was ordained, I had the good fortune of attending a weekend preaching seminar led by the late Father Charles Miller, CM, who at the time taught homiletics at St. John's Seminary in Los Angeles, California. At that seminar, I heard for the first time the term *contemplative preacher*. I was struck by that phrase and I think it is a good description of what we should be aiming at as deacons. According to Father Miller, it means that we must be aware at all times of the bits and pieces of homilies we are encountering every day of our lives. Father Miller's mantra was, "There's a homily in everything."

I am reminded of the opening lines of Thomas Merton's classic, *Seeds of Contemplation:* "Every moment and every event of every man's life on earth plants something in his soul. For just as the wind carries thousands of invisible and visible winged seeds, so the stream of time brings with it germs of spiritual vitality that come to rest imperceptibly in the minds and wills of men."[1]

That is the thought I had in mind in preparing this set of homilies for Cycle A of the liturgical year—to gather together some of the seeds of everyday experience and try my best to interpret them in the light of the gospel. The result is this collection of homilies. One of the first seeds I came across was the messages found on many Christmas cards that arrive in mid-Advent and seem so premature in their greeting. And so in the first homily of this book, entitled "Advent Cards," I play with the idea of sending cards with a true Advent message. Reflection on this ordinary seasonal experience led to a homily that challenges the listener to really take seriously the time of expectant waiting we call Advent.

I found another seed marvelously woven into a poem by the great Jesuit poet, Gerard Manley Hopkins, "God's Grandeur." It is a beautiful poem, one filled with images capable of expressing all the meaning of Christmas, and one I used for Homily No. 7 at Midnight Christmas Mass, entitled "You Are the Grandeur of God." Most of us will never attain the level of a poet like Hopkins, but we should certainly not hesitate to use such great works to capture the meaning of one of the most significant moments in salvation history—the incarnation. And the great thing about poems like "God's Grandeur" is that they have a surplus of meaning. You may take the poem, as well as the ideas developed in the homily, and weave them into a suitable message for just about any Sunday or feast day of the year. Are not the saints also reflective of the grandeur of God?

One of the places in which I frequently find seeds for contemplative preaching is good movies. Admittedly, it takes some searching to find a good one, but from time to time one comes along that cries out for inclusion in a homily. One of those films is *Babette's Feast*, which in my judgment should be required viewing during diaconate formation when the subject is the Eucharist. I tried to capture some of those eucharistic overtones in Homily No. 39, "Come, Taste the Fine Food and Enjoy." The first thing that this homily has going for it is that it tells a story—a love story really—a story of love that has grown cold and diminished. I believe that as you read it you will see the possibilities for rekindling love in a community, starting with the sharing of ordinary food, and rising to the level of extraordinary nourishment in the body and blood of Christ.

One of the pieces of advice I still remember from Father Miller was his declaration that "a contemplative is always preparing a homily." He stressed that every time you hear someone preach, ask yourself, "How would I preach that?" I encourage you to do that with these homilies. I would be pleased someday to hear another deacon—priest or bishop, too, for that matter—taking some of the ideas found in this book and preaching them in a new way, a unique way, a more contemplative way. The seeds are there. Don't let them lie idle. Take them into your hearts and minds; let them grow in the good soil of contemplation until they bring forth excellent fruit.

PART ONE

Advent

HOMILIES 1–5

Celebrating Advent means being able to wait. Waiting, however, is an art that our impatient age has forgotten.... We must wait for the greatest, most profound, most gentle things in the world; nothing happens in a rush, but only according to the divine laws of germination and growth and becoming.

Dietrich Bonhoeffer, *Christmas with Dietrich Bonhoeffer*[1]

1
ADVENT CARDS
First Sunday of Advent (A)

- Isaiah 2:1–5
- Romans 13:11–14
- Matthew 24:37–44

I have been thinking of starting a new tradition and would like to get your feedback on it this morning. The idea I have is for a new line of greeting cards—*Advent* cards. You see, I have become disenchanted with traditional Christmas greeting cards. They always arrive during Advent, not during the octave of Christmas, and, more importantly, they never carry the message we should be hearing during these weeks of Advent.

You know what I mean. All of us will soon receive Christmas cards with messages that say, "Merry Christmas...Have a joyous Christmas... Happy Holidays...Joyeux Noël!" Now, let's be clear: I have nothing against these messages. It's just that they are incomplete. And premature. Before we can truly find meaning in messages of peace and joy, we have to hear the sharp, no-nonsense, cut-to-the-bone message of the prophets, telling us to prepare for the approaching joy of Christ's birth.

So, I have in mind a line of Advent cards. In fact, I have already designed several of them. The first one has a picture of John the Baptist on the front. He is gaunt, sunburned, dressed in camel-hair clothing; he looks like someone who has been living on locusts and wild honey. The greeting on the front of the card says, "Repent!" When you open the card, the message continues: "That your heart may be as pure as the Christ Child on Christmas Day!" What do you think of that?

The second card I have designed is based on today's Gospel. It features Jesus on the front, looking somewhat less austere than John the Baptist, but with a mixture of sternness and compassion on his face. The greeting reads, "Stay awake!" On the inside it says, "That you may discover the Christ Child in the faces of the poor and forgotten!"

So, what do you think? Will this idea catch on? Would you welcome such an Advent card in your mailbox during the next several weeks?

If you answer in the negative—and I would not be offended if you do—it is probably because we have little appreciation for the words of the prophets. We heard one of the greatest of them in the first reading from Isaiah. Again, in the Gospel from Matthew, Jesus is speaking in a prophetic voice. And he isn't saying, "Have a Merry Christmas!" He is saying, "Be ready! Be prepared!" That is the essential message we must hear during this season of Advent. We have to be shaken out of our lethargy, awakened from our unreal dreams, separated from our preoccupation with presents and parties; all of this so that hope and compassion may be rekindled in our hearts, our minds, our consciousness. Then, we will arrive at Christmas morning ready not only to greet the Christ Child in the manger but to experience his being born in us.

In Old Testament times, the prophets did this very well. Unfortunately, the voices of the Old Testament prophets are pretty much foreign to our ears. We hear an occasional reading at Mass, but we miss the core message. We miss the strident, unequivocal voices of Amos, Hosea, Isaiah, each of them proclaiming a message of warning and…a message of hope.

To bridge the gap between our world and the world of the prophets, I have consulted someone who knew the prophets well. One of the best authorities on this subject is Rabbi Abraham J. Heschel, who wrote the classic two volume work, *The Prophets*.[2]

Heschel shows us why the words of the prophets would seem so out of place on a twenty-first-century greeting card. He says that the prophets were dismayed about things that we accept as normal:

> To us a single act of injustice—cheating in business, exploitation of the poor—is slight; to the prophets, a disaster. To us injustice is injurious to the welfare of the people; to the prophets it is a death-blow to existence; to us an episode; to them, a catastrophe, a threat to the world.

> Their breathless impatience with injustice may strike us as hysteria. We ourselves witness continually acts of injustice, manifestations of hypocrisy, falsehood, outrage, misery, but we rarely grow indignant or overly excited. To the prophets even a minor injustice assumes cosmic proportions.[3]

Injustice, falsehood, hypocrisy are just as real today as in the days of Isaiah, but we rarely grow indignant or overly excited. The prophets spoke to people just like ourselves whose sensitivity to evil and sin were sometimes as dulled as our own. The Israelites had their idols, we have our televisions; they had their affluence in the midst of poverty, we have the same—statistics show a steadily widening gap between the rich and the poor in this country. It was to awaken people to this reality that the prophets raged. It is the same reason Jesus says in today's Gospel, "Stay awake!"

Heschel goes on to say:

> The prophet is human, yet he employs notes one octave too high for our ears. He experiences moments that defy our understanding. He is neither "a singing saint" nor "a moralizing poet," but an assaulter of the mind. Often his words begin to burn where conscience ends.[4]

Why does the prophet employ notes one octave too high for our ears? It is because he is on fire with love and compassion. Heschel says:

> Almost every prophet brings consolation, promise and the hope of reconciliation along with censure and castigation. He begins with *a message of doom*; he concludes with a *message of hope.*[5] [emphasis in the original]

Thus, Isaiah can exclaim:

> Shout out, do not hold back!
> Lift up your voice like a trumpet!
> Announce to my people their rebellion,
>   to the house of Jacob their sins. (Isa 58:1 NRSV)

But he also speaks the beautiful, hope-filled words of today's first reading:

> They shall beat their swords into plowshares
>   and their spears into pruning hooks;
> one nation shall not raise the sword against another,
>   nor shall they train for war again.
> O house of Jacob, come,
>   let us walk in the light of the LORD. (Isa 2:4–5)

The prophets knew what we should know even better in our Christian era—God is not far from us. The God who is transcendent and mysterious is also very near, very much present in the ordinary. But we cannot realize this unless we are awake. The message of Advent is a plea, a plea that this year we will "awake from sleep," as St. Paul says (Rom 13:11). If the message sounds harsh or disturbing, it is because the prophet knows how much we have to gain by waking up. It is, finally, a message of hope. It is the hope of Advent: that we will awaken and live in a world cultivated by plowshares and pruning hooks, rather than a world ravaged by swords and spears. That is the hope of Advent.

Wake up and claim it!

Questions for Further Discussion:

1. If you were designing an Advent card, what message would you put on it? How do you think it would be received?

2. Can you name any prophets today? What does it mean to employ notes "one octave too high for our ears"?

2
MARY, MODEL OF PERFECT FREEDOM
Feast of the Immaculate Conception (A)

- Genesis 3:9–15, 20
- Ephesians 1:3–6, 11–12
- Luke 1:26–38

During a recent class in our Rite of Christian Initiation for Adults (RCIA), I asked the participants about their understanding of the Immaculate Conception. I was not surprised when catechumens did not know the significance of this Catholic teaching, but I was disappointed when catechized Catholics responded that it had something to do with the conception of Jesus without human sexual relations and, therefore, without sin.

Perhaps a partial explanation for this confusion is the passage from Luke's Gospel that we just heard. The Gospel reading is *not* about *Mary's* conception, which is nowhere mentioned in the gospels, but about *Jesus* being conceived by the power of the Holy Spirit. We simply do not have a scriptural basis for the doctrine of the Immaculate Conception, which was declared by Pope Pius IX in 1854.

Nevertheless, there is a seed of this great truth in the Gospel that can, through theological reflection, lead us to a deeper appreciation of Mary's holiness. And this reflection can help us experience more fully the operation of grace in our lives leading us to that same holiness.

The starting point for this reflection is Mary's response to the angel's announcement that she would conceive and bear the Son of God. Mary says simply: "Behold, I am the handmaid of the Lord. May it be done to me according to your word" (Luke 1:38). In this humble response, Mary revealed something about herself that grounds our belief in her Immaculate Conception. Mary's *fiat*, her willingness to accept whatever God intended for her, points to her perfect acceptance of the gift God gives to every person: the gift of freedom. By accepting God's will for her without reservation, Mary revealed her true perfection.

If freedom is the greatest gift God gives to humankind, then original sin might be thought of as the abuse of that freedom. As representatives of our race, Adam and Eve symbolize the perfect freedom God intended for all humankind. But we believe that in some way that perfect freedom was abused. In contrast, Mary *never* abused the freedom given to her by God. Mary is, therefore, the model of perfect freedom. She *is* the Immaculate Conception.

The theologian Hans Urs von Balthasar speaks of three dimensions of the acceptance of God's gift of infinite freedom: thanksgiving, prayer, and divine indwelling.[6] When we are fully open to God's gift of freedom, we naturally respond in gratitude. Mary's gratitude is expressed in the verses that follow right after today's Gospel reading. In Mary's canticle, or Magnificat, Mary's gratitude for her own giftedness can be heard: "My soul magnifies the Lord, and my spirit rejoices in God my Savior, for he has looked with favor on the lowliness of his servant. Surely, from now on all generations will call me blessed" (Luke 1:46–48 NRSV). The essence of the Magnificat is that God has done this great wonder. To Mary it is *all* gift. And her rejoicing expresses her gratitude to God.

The next dimension Balthasar explores is that of prayer. He says prayer is "the most tangible realization of human freedom."[7] We pray as Jesus did, trusting in God's will. For Catholics, there is no better model for prayer than Mary. The centuries of devotion to Mary as companion and intercessor in prayer are overwhelming testimony to Mary's perfect acceptance of the gift of freedom.

Finally, Balthasar reflects on God's indwelling in those who have accepted the gift of freedom. When we have accepted that gift, Christ is born in us. Is it any wonder, then, that Christ should have been conceived in Mary, since she was perfect in her acceptance of the gift of freedom?

Questions for Further Discussion:

1. Are you able to see freedom as God's greatest gift to us? How do you experience that freedom?

2. How is Mary a model for the perfect use of freedom? How is freedom abused?

3
NOW THAT I HAVE YOUR ATTENTION
Second Sunday of Advent (A)

- Isaiah 11:1–10
- Romans 15:4–9
- Matthew 3:1–12

My friend, Deacon Lynn Johnson, who for many years was assigned to the Cathedral of the Madeleine in Salt Lake City, told me a story recently that applies to today's Gospel. It wasn't until I had thought about this story for a while that I realized it is an Advent story.

Once Lynn was serving as deacon of the Mass at the cathedral and had just finished proclaiming the gospel. As he did so, he noticed a young woman in a miniskirt, cell phone on her hip, walking up the aisle toward the sanctuary. She stopped in front of the pulpit, stared up at Deacon Lynn, and then said in a loud voice, "You're a liar!"

Lynn said he stood transfixed for some time, his face turning a bright red. The eyes of everyone in the cathedral were riveted on this strange scene. Then, the woman turned and walked away. When he recovered, Lynn said, "Now that I have your attention, let me begin my homily."

Since I first heard this story, I have wondered how I might have reacted. Of course, if I had my wits about me, I might have said: "Madam, I believe you are judging by appearances. I may appear to be a liar but, in fact, I am a lawyer. The two are not necessarily the same."

But this is an *Advent* story, because it reminds us of John the Baptist, who, in today's Gospel, comes out of nowhere, strides onto the scene in an unusual costume, and says some pretty shocking things. He certainly must have gotten the attention of the good people of Jerusalem, Judea, and the region around the Jordan when he called the Pharisees and Sadducees: a "brood of vipers." John uses equally strong language when he speaks of the one who is to come after him. Jesus of Nazareth, he says, will come gathering his wheat into his barn, and burning the chaff with unquenchable fire.

Strong stuff. But Advent is supposed to be that way. I have been reading lately *The Prison Meditations of Father Alfred Delp*.[8] Father Delp was a German convert to Catholicism, a Jesuit who was imprisoned and executed by the Nazis. In his prison meditations, he says that Advent is a time for rousing. It is a time when we must be shaken to our very depths, a time of renunciation and surrender. He says it is only when the framework is shaken that real life begins.[9]

For many Americans a kind of Advent began, not last Sunday, but on September 11, 2001. That was the day the framework was shaken and many began to realize the possibility of real life. For some, it was the attraction of a simpler lifestyle, the importance of family and friends. For others, it was a reminder of the impermanence of life, of what former Beatle, the late George Harrison, sang about in *All Things Must Pass*. But it was a shaking of the framework, a true Advent experience.

And so perhaps the miniskirted intruder in the cathedral sanctuary was a reminder that we need at times to be shocked and shaken to our depths. And perhaps the strange appearance I just described is an invitation to ask: Do we as Catholic Christians appear to the world as liars?

And I think that if we are honest with ourselves, we have to answer, at least in part: *Yes*. I do not mean that we purposely lie. What I mean is that the truth we have been given is too much for us to comprehend and express; it simply exceeds our human capacity.

During Advent we prepare for the coming of God into our world: the God who made the universe, who put the stars in their places and set the planets in motion; the God who made the Pleiades and Orion, who created the leopard and the lamb, the lion and the calf; the God who created all of this, we believe, has chosen to become one of us. If I live to be a hundred, and if I were to preach every Sunday, I would never be able to give adequate expression to that great wonder.

And so, to those on the outside looking in, yes, we must appear to be telling lies, or at least half-truths, fibs about reality. We appear as liars because it is difficult to express and to put into practice the great truths we profess to believe. When we consider what God has done for us, we must appear as impostors, even hypocrites. We proclaim that God has become human, that we have been freed from slavery to sin, and yet our efforts to free others from the slavery of poverty, disease, and oppression fall so woefully short of what our world needs.

We find ourselves unable to apply the truth we profess as Catholics, even though we have available to us the best-developed teaching on social justice of any religious tradition. We have been given gospel-based principles, well-reasoned arguments, carefully articulated statements on social justice, but for the most part, they remain a secret to but a few. Rather than discoursing with the world using our language of social justice, we enter into this important conversation sounding much like the rest of society. The world is waiting for us as Catholics to claim the truth that has been given us.

Advent is a time for rousing, but a very special kind of rousing. It is a time for rousing ourselves to *new hope*. We find that hope in the Gospel. John the Baptist uses strong language, extreme language. But John the Baptist did not get it quite right. He seems to anticipate a *merciless* messiah, someone who will burn the chaff with unquenchable fire. If we stopped reading the Gospel at this point, there would seem to be *no* hope. We have to read on. We know the beginning, the middle, and the end of this story. John did not. We know that Jesus was *always* merciful, that the bruised reed he would not break, and the smoldering wick he would not quench. Jesus knew our nature. He knew that our capacity for truth must be stretched and expanded over a lifetime. He knew that it takes a lifetime for us to live out fully what we profess to believe.

And so the final word to the woman in the miniskirt has to be this: Yes, we appear as liars, but God is not finished with us. We are works in progress, unfinished masterpieces. And when those individual masterpieces are completed, they will give full expression to the truth and beauty that is Christ. That will be the glory of God. And that is no lie.

Questions for Further Discussion:

1. What aspect of the truth we have been given do you find the hardest to articulate? Which is the hardest to live out in your life?

2. Have you felt your capacity for truth being stretched and expanded? How?

4

NO PRISON CAN KEEP OUT
THE LIGHT OF CHRIST
Third Sunday of Advent (A)

> • Isaiah 35:1–6a, 10
> • James 5:7–10
> • Matthew 11:2–11

A prison is a dark and fearful place where even a holy man may lose sight of God.

A prison is a lonely place where even a prophet may no longer hear the voice of God.

But no prison is so dark, so fearful, or so lonely that it cannot be penetrated by the light of Christ.

John the Baptist, perhaps the greatest prophet of all time, with one foot in the Old Testament and one in the New, suddenly finds himself in a dark and fearful prison.

John the Baptist, the prophet described by Jesus as the greatest of those born of woman, has begun to question what he saw and heard of Jesus.

John the Baptist, the man who saw the Holy Spirit descend like a dove on Jesus, the one whose sandal he was not worthy to untie, now utters the question that echoes down through the centuries and reverberates in our own hearts: "Are you the one who is to come, or should we look for another?"

That same question, or some variation of it, is in our minds this Third Sunday of Advent. But, more importantly, we are beginning to dimly perceive the answer.

The answer that Jesus sent to John in prison was one that John could not have misunderstood, for it echoed the words of the prophet Isaiah: the One who is to come, the Christ, will open the eyes of the blind, cause the deaf to hear, the lame to leap, the mute to sing. When we witness these miracles in the prisons of our own lives, then we have heard the answer to the perennial question: Are you the one who is to come or should we look for another?

We sometimes find ourselves in little prisons that are as real and as confining as the one that held John the Baptist. You young people— you may find yourselves at times confined by the prison of peer pressure, pressure to conform, to be someone other than yourself. And mothers and fathers—do we not at times find ourselves imprisoned by fears and worries about our children? Will they succeed, will they have faith, will they even survive in this hostile world? And as we all inevitably approach old age, we face the very real prison of declining health, of growing dependence on others, on confinement in a nursing home or hospital bed. These are real prisons; we should not pretend they do not exist.

The Church does not promise us that Advent will tear down these prison walls; it *does* teach us that, if we are faithful during Advent, these walls will be penetrated by the light of Christ.

How does this happen? The Church admonishes us to remember. Remember the times in our lives when the word of God came to us as it did to John the Baptist in prison; remember when the experience of God produced in us a light that dispelled the darkness and enabled us to again see clearly. Remember those fleeting moments when we experienced a long, loving look at the divine that came gratuitously, leaving us with an abiding sense of peace and assurance. Remember a time when the words of Julian of Norwich, herself a voluntary prisoner for Christ, resonated with us: "But all will be well and all will be well and every manner of thing will be well."[10]

Did John the Baptist remember such moments? The testimony of other prisoners convinces me that he did. The late Egyptian president, Anwar Sadat, who was himself once a political prisoner, said that confinement drives some men insane, others it turns into saints. One of those probable saints is the German Jesuit, Father Alfred Delp. Father Delp was a convert to Catholicism, taken into custody by the Nazis in 1944 for being part of a group that was discussing how to rebuild Germany along Christian lines. Before his execution on February 2, 1945, Father Delp left us some beautiful reflections on the season of Advent. On the Third Sunday of Advent, 1944, he wrote from prison:

> [E]very now and then my whole being is flooded with pulsating life and my heart can scarcely contain the delirious joy there is in it. Suddenly, without any cause that I can perceive, without knowing why or by what right, my spirits soar again and there is not a doubt in my mind that all the promises hold good.... There are times when one is curiously uplifted by a sense of inner exaltation and comfort. Outwardly nothing is changed. The hopelessness of the situation remains only too obvious; yet one can face it undismayed. One is content to leave everything in God's hands.[11]

These are words that suggest the answer we are seeking, for they describe the experience of Christ coming to us in whatever prison we may find ourselves. No prison can keep out the light of Christ; the prisons that held John the Baptist, St. Peter, St. Paul, St. John of the Cross, Father Delp, Martin Luther King, Dorothy Day—not one of them could hold out the light of Christ. There is no prison, no matter how dark, how fearful, how lonely, that cannot be penetrated by the light of Christ. And if Christ can be found in such prisons, surely he will be found in our lives this Advent season…if we let him.

Father Delp has a further thought on Advent. He says:

> Advent is the time for rousing.… A shattering awakening; that is the necessary preliminary. Life only begins when the whole framework is shaken.… We have to listen, to keep watch, to let our heart quicken under the impulse of the indwelling Spirit.[12]

If we allow ourselves to be roused, and if we remember, then we will know why the Church says to us on this Third Sunday—*Rejoice!* This is the traditional Gaudete Sunday, when the Church says to us unequivocally and emphatically—*Rejoice!* Why? Because the Church knows that joy is the natural fruit of a good Advent.

Rejoice, then! Already the rose-candled dawn appears in the eastern sky. The darkness has lost its power. In the words of Shakespeare:

> Some say, that ever 'gainst that season comes
> Wherein our Savior's birth is celebrated
> The bird of dawning singeth all night long;
> The nights are wholesome; then no planets strike,
> No fairy takes, nor witch hath power to charm;
> So hallow'd and so gracious is the time. (Hamlet Act I, scene i)

Rejoice, for, indeed, hallowed and gracious is the time.

Questions for Further Discussion:

1. What prisons are you concerned about this Advent season?
2. In what do you rejoice this Gaudete Sunday?

5
BEHOLD!
Fourth Sunday of Advent (A)

- Isaiah 7:10–14
- Romans 1:1–7
- Matthew 1:18–24

In the fourth century of the Church, many Christians left the cities and went out into the desert to live holy lives. We sometimes refer to them as the desert fathers and mothers. These holy men and women left us a collection of words of advice intended for those who came asking how to live a holy life. Typically, someone would come to one of the abbas or ammas and say, "Give me a word that I might find salvation." They would often receive some strange-sounding advice, such as, "Go to your monastic cell and stay there. Your cell will teach you everything."

If we were to go to Matthew or to Luke during this season of Advent and ask for a word by which we might find salvation, the word we might be given is *Behold!* Today's Gospel says, "Behold, the virgin shall conceive and bear a son…"(Matt 1:23). What is the significance of this command to behold? What does it mean?

It means, first of all, to pay attention. Something important is about to happen. Wake up! Be aware! Don't miss the importance of this event! Today, we might say, "May I have your attention, please. Listen up! Hello, people!"

On this Fourth Sunday of Advent, we need to hear this word *Behold* on a very deep level, because our human nature keeps us in a state of forgetfulness, of semiconsciousness. We need to be awakened again and again to the utter strangeness of what is about to happen—God becomes human! We are about to ponder anew that Mary gave birth to the one who created her! That is, indeed, a strange idea, a foreign concept. Unless we make a real effort to pay attention, the strangeness of what we proclaim will be lost in a kind of unthinking, unreflective familiarity. Ho, hum, God has become incarnate, big deal.

Joseph in today's Gospel experienced that strangeness in a disturbing way. To discover that Mary was with child was not only strange, it was scandalous. The Gospel records that Joseph learned through a dream that he was to *embrace* this strangeness, to take it into his home. The Gospel, which unfolds throughout the life of Jesus from the incarnation to the resurrection, will always seem strange. Our willingness to take in that strangeness and give it a home in our hearts determines our spiritual health, our salvation.

The word that will give us salvation is, *Behold!* Look closely.

An unbelieving world deals with the strangeness of the incarnation by simply ignoring it. To the unbeliever, the notion of a virgin conceiving a son and naming him Emmanuel, God Is with Us, is so absurd that it need not be pondered. It can be safely ignored. Our response on the other hand may be something like this: "It is written in the Bible. It is a doctrine of the Church. We Catholics believe it. Besides, it's a mystery."

On one level that may be an adequate response to what we are about to celebrate. But it is a response formed primarily out of our physical consciousness. The better response—the response the Church strives for during this season—is a response shaped by our spiritual consciousness. That is the level of consciousness we must operate out of, if we are to experience deeply the truth of the incarnation.

How to get there? How to live more fully out of a spiritual consciousness? Again, the word we are given is *Behold!*

One way of describing trinitarian life is as a loving gaze, a glance of love, among the Persons of the Trinity. The Father looks upon the Son, the Son gazes lovingly at the Father, and from their loving gaze proceeds the Holy Spirit whose glance in turn is directed toward the Father and the Son.

We participate in this activity of the Trinity through our life in the Church. Our adoration, our prayers of petition, our thanksgiving in the Eucharist are all forms of participation in trinitarian life. We may call that participation *contemplation.* And the more we join in the trinitarian life, the more our own spiritual consciousness will be awakened. Then, what once seemed strange becomes real and true; what once seemed scandalous is seen as redemptive.

There is one more thing that must be said about the mutually loving gaze of trinitarian life: It begets action. The same is true for us. As we adore more deeply the God who is to be born in us at Christmas, a desire arises to care for others. We may call this *contemplation in action.* We experience a renewed desire to care for the body of Christ, wherever that care is needed. Having experienced the birth of Christ in our own hearts, we become midwives to others who have yet to experience him.

When we ponder Mary and Joseph far from home in a strange land, we remember the unwelcome immigrant, the homeless among us. When we gaze lovingly upon the baby Jesus in the manger, our contemplation moves us to action; we look for ways to relieve the suffering of children in our community and throughout the world. To look lovingly is to experience compassion.

There is one final place in scripture where we are enjoined to behold or to see. It occurs in the Book of Revelation, the last book of the Bible. There, Christ says, "See, I am making all things new" (Rev 21:5 NRSV). That is what Christ wills for us at the close of Advent: to be so awake, so aware that what we are about to experience is breathtakingly new.

We do not need to go to the desert this morning to ask for a word that will bring us salvation. The word is here in today's Gospel: *Behold!*

Questions For Further Discussion:

1. Is there another word besides *Behold* that appeals to you as a word of salvation during Advent? What would it be?

2. How does your contemplation during Advent lead you to action?

PART TWO
Christmas Season
HOMILIES 6–13

The Lord, whose compassion we want to manifest in time and place,
is indeed the displaced Lord. Paul describes Jesus as the one who
voluntarily displaced himself: "His state was divine, yet he did not
cling to his equality with God but emptied himself to assume the
condition of a slave, and became as we are." A greater displacement
cannot be conceived. The mystery of the incarnation is that God
assumed the condition of a suffering human being. Thus,
God became a displaced God to whom nothing human was alien,
a God who could fully experience the brokenness of our human
condition.... Jesus Christ is the displaced Lord in whom God's
compassion becomes flesh. In him we see a life of displacement lived
to the fullest. It is in following our displaced Lord that
the Christian community is formed.

Henri J. M. Nouwen, Donald P. McNeill, Douglas A. Morrison,
Compassion: A Reflection on the Christian Life[1]

6
WHY JOSEPH DREAMED
Christmas Vigil (A)

- Isaiah 62:1–5
- Acts 13:16–17, 22–25
- Matthew 1:1–25

Joseph was a righteous man who slept the sleep of the just.

Joseph was a working man who knew the satisfaction of rest, of deep, restorative sleep after a hard day's work.

Joseph was not a man who tossed and turned, who counted sheep, or who went to the medicine cabinet for a sleeping aid.

Joseph was a man accustomed to undisturbed sleep.

But this night, the night described in the Gospel, was an exception. It is fair to infer that Joseph, like any good and sensitive man, had not been sleeping well. His betrothed, his Mary, was in serious danger. To be found pregnant out of wedlock was a capital offense in Joseph's time. For Joseph who loved Mary, this reality alone was enough to make him restless.

But there was more. We just heard the long genealogy starting with Abraham, running down through centuries of Jewish history, through Judah and Tamar, Boaz and Ruth, David and the wife of Uriah, reaching its climax in Joseph, the husband of Mary. There was a tremendous weight of ancestry bearing down on the sleepless Joseph that night. Each of those ancestors had lived with the certainty of death, the fear natural to a man that his life might not be continued in offspring. Each of them dealt with the fear of death in a fundamentally human way—by having children. Thus it was that Josiah became the father of Jeconiah, Achim the father of Eliud. Each new birth, each new descendant, did something to allay the fear every man has of passing out of existence.

And now on the weight of Joseph's rugged shoulders rested the dilemma: to put aside his betrothed Mary and jeopardize his posterity or take her in, despite the cloud that hung over her. And so he spent his sleepless night, recalling his ancestry and his own natural desire for descendants.

But there were even more thoughts tugging at his mind that night. There was the hope expressed in Isaiah that Jerusalem would be vindicated, that kings would see the glory of Jerusalem restored. There was the promise that Joseph's people would no longer be called forsaken but, rather, "My Delight," and the land of his ancestors, "Espoused." The hope that this would come about now depended on Joseph. Joseph turned over in his mind the thought expressed by Paul in the second reading: the savior, the Messiah, would come from the House of David. He was of the House of David. And he was faced with a terrible dilemma.

Is it any wonder that Joseph was not sleeping well that night?

It is said that man's extremity is God's opportunity. When we are in extreme circumstances—a sudden life-threatening illness, impending death—there is an opportunity for God to break through our complacency. Joseph was in extreme circumstances. And in this sleep-deprived state something happened that is very human—he began to dream. The dream was God's opportunity.

From that dream Joseph received assurance, and, perhaps through later reflection, he realized a truth we still struggle to make a part of our consciousness. He learned that neither he nor anyone else need fear death ever again. This child that Mary was carrying would put an end to death. No longer was there the desperate need for offspring. For the first time in history, the possibility was presented of *living completely without fear.* From now on men and women called by God could embrace virginity, for they would know that real life is propagated and perpetuated through Jesus Christ, *not* through descendants.

Joseph's dream would show to him, and to those who believed in the gospel, that the longing for a messiah as a consolation in the face of death was now fulfilled. Joseph and those who came after him could live in the utter joy and freedom of knowing God is with us: *Emmanuel.*

In the nights that followed, Joseph slept like a baby, because of the baby. The baby Jesus, that is. Once again, he slept the sleep of the just. He slept that way at least until the next crisis in his life, when Jesus became a teenager. But even then he did not need a dream to remind him of what he knew well—*God is with us!* No human event, not even Golgotha, could change that.

When this vigil ends, my friends, go to your homes and sleep well. Sleep well, because in the morning the one who has taken away the fear of death will be born. If you dream, may it be dreams of Christmas, of promises fulfilled, of the comforting knowledge that God is truly with us.

Questions for Further Discussion:

1. Do you think that God still speaks to people in dreams? If not, how does God speak to you?

2. Do you see the coming of God among us in Christ as removing the fear of death?

7
YOU ARE THE GRANDEUR OF GOD
Christmas Midnight (A)

- Isaiah 9:1–6
- Titus 2:11–14
- Luke 2:1–14

There is a sacredness to this night unrivaled by any other night. It is a night filled with anticipation of what will be revealed here. It is a night when nature is at her best, for tonight nature—human nature—is revealed as the dwelling place of God.

We sing, "Silent Night, Holy Night" with a sense of awe and expectation at the beauty about to be experienced here. Nature is prepared to reveal a beauty not easily captured in words, a beauty better left to the graced hands of poets. And so we turn to a poet, to someone especially gifted by God to shape language into a precious chalice of words suitable for carrying the meaning of this night.

Perhaps the poet who can bring us closest to the threshold of meaning we find in this night is the Jesuit poet Gerard Manley Hopkins, who, in a poem entitled "God's Grandeur," wrote:

> The world is charged with the grandeur of God.
>   It will flame out, like shining from shook foil;
>   It gathers to a greatness, like the ooze of oil
> Crushed. Why do men then now not reck his rod?
> Generations have trod, have trod, have trod;
>   And all is seared with trade; bleared, smeared with toil;
>   And wears man's smudge and shares man's smell: the soil
> Is bare now, nor can foot feel, being shod.
>
> And for all this, nature is never spent;
>   There lives the dearest freshness deep down things;

> And though the last lights off the black West went
>   Oh, morning, at the brown brink eastward, springs—
> Because the Holy Ghost over the bent
>   World broods with warm breast and with ah! bright wings.[2]

Tonight, our Advent preparation completed, we marvel at the grandeur of God, not just the surface features of nature but "the dearest freshness deep down things." I mean the ultimate expression of God's grandeur—our own human nature that, on this night, was united forever with the divine.

We sit, or stand as the case may be, like the shepherds in the fields, dazzled by bright angels, revealing to mortals something hinted at for centuries—a savior has been born for you who is Christ and Lord! This is the secret hidden in human nature: Tonight, God is at home in humankind. This is the "the dearest freshness deep down things" that tonight glimmers and dazzles like shook foil. This is the message of the angel, spoken two thousand years ago and repeated again and again—a savior has been born for you who is Christ and Lord!

Only an angel could speak this message to humankind, for it came from God. What the shepherds saw that night was a brilliant ray of light from the face of God, yet veiled, as it must be, by an angel, for no one can see God and live. The light of God must necessarily be veiled, for we humans could not stand its intensity. And so this same light has been veiled in nature, in the intricate fashioning of creatures whose infinite variety hints of a divine Creator. This light has been veiled in scripture, in the prophets, those who not only spoke for, but counseled with, God. This divine light glows in the words of Isaiah: "For a child is born to us, a son is given us; upon his shoulder dominion rests. They name him Wonder-Counselor, God-Hero, Father-Forever, Prince of Peace" (Isa 9:6). The light of God is veiled, even in the child lying in the manger. By becoming incarnate, God accommodated our limited capacity for bearing the light of truth.

And what is this truth that on this night dazzles shepherds, excites the heavenly host, keeps ordinary folks like ourselves awake past midnight? It is this: God values human nature. You see, one of the sad legacies we have received from centuries of people who never glimpsed the grandeur of God is a kind of cheapened valuing of what it means to be human. As the poet says, "generations have trod, have trod, have trod...." And all that treading has produced a general sense that we humans are really not worth much. Tonight, that sad conclusion is blasted away by this Christmas truth—we, you and I, *are* the grandeur of God! That is the simple, yet absolutely true, message you must take home with you tonight. You are the grandeur of God! Don't leave here without it—you are the grandeur of God!

Say it with me, "I am the grandeur of God!" Get used to it. It will change your life.

I have a theory as to why this fundamental truth comes with such reluctance to our lips. My theory is this: The same dark spirit that lurks on the edges of this Gospel scene, the dark spirit that would follow Jesus to Good Friday, to Golgotha, also seeks to deprive you of what is your most priceless inheritance—a deep, unshakable awareness that *you* are the grandeur of God.

In the days and weeks, the months and the years, that follow this night, that dark spirit will obscure the light you have glimpsed here. It will whisper to you in moments of weakness that you are no more than a biological entity, that the still, small voice of God that speaks to you in prayer, in devotion, is but a psychological notion; that the pull you feel to turn away from sin and to live a new life is an illusion. That evil spirit will do this to weaken the power you receive by being here this night. It will try to drive from your memory what is declared to you this night: *You* are the grandeur of God!

God so loved human nature that God became manifest in us. I would not even say that God chose humankind among other choices. I would say that God *could do nothing other* than become incarnate. God did this because God is comfortable in human skin. God did not have to try on human nature like a new coat and decide whether it was comfortable, whether it looked good. God was with us from the start. But tonight it is manifested for all to see.

God is at home in the human heart. God finds wild, intoxicating joy in every good human activity. Every good thought, every tiny prayer, every gentle melody hummed while at work delights the God who lives in you. Every good thing you do is a tiny note in the chorus of human nature singing of the grandeur of God.

God finds hope in what humankind can do, once it realizes its own dignity. We give God hope when we leave behind a passive acceptance of evil and enter, instead, into partnership with God, using all our talents, all our energy, all our imagination to bring about a world that befits a people who reflect the grandeur of God. Come awake this evening, although the hour is late, and claim the dignity that is yours.

Questions for Further Discussion:

1. In what way are *you* "the grandeur of God"?
2. What keeps us from realizing this truth?

8

THE SHEPHERDS' GOSPEL
Christmas Dawn (A)

- Isaiah 62:11–12
- Titus 3:4–7
- Luke 2:15–20

What was Mary pondering that first Christmas morning? Luke says, "And Mary kept all these things, reflecting on them in her heart" (Luke 2:19). What were her thoughts as she listened to the rough shepherds glorifying and praising God?

Everyone who hears this Christmas Gospel will likely have a different idea. But I want to suggest one possibility this Christmas dawn. Perhaps Mary was reflecting on what she had proclaimed some months earlier when she visited Elizabeth. In what we call "Mary's Canticle" we hear these words:

> My soul magnifies the Lord,
>   and my spirit rejoices in God my Savior....
> He has shown strength with his arm;
>   he has scattered the proud in the thoughts of their hearts.
> He has brought down the powerful from their thrones,
>   and lifted up the lowly. (Luke 1:46–47, 51–52 NRSV)

Perhaps Mary saw in the shepherds the fulfillment of her own words—the powerful are deposed and the lowly lifted up.

In Luke's Gospel, the birth of Jesus begins with the powerful and ends with the powerless. Events are set in motion by the high and mighty, but those same events receive their meaning from the lowly. Mary's Canticle resounds in the fields outside Bethlehem, just as it will later at Tepeyac Hill near Mexico City, and as it does in our own world.

Last night, at Midnight Mass, we listened to the opening lines of Luke, chapter 2, and we heard that "a decree went out from Caesar Augustus that the whole world should be enrolled" (Luke 2:1). Caesar

Augustus was a powerful man. One word and people stopped what they were doing, traveled long distances and willingly submitted to be counted. Luke adds that the enrollment was the first to be ordered while Quirinius was governor of Syria. Again, a powerful figure no doubt. But Luke's account ends not with the privileged but with the lowly. It ends with the shepherds, those lowly representatives of the common folk who seem to enjoy a special place in God's eyes.

At the time of Jesus' birth, shepherds were about as lowly as you could get. They were the peasants, the common folk, people who may even have been a little outside the law. One scholar says they could not testify in judicial proceedings, apparently because they were prone to breaking the law by grazing their herds where they didn't belong.[3]

But, still, they were the class of people chosen to first hear the good news—God has come among us. God has become incarnate. God is with us. The shepherds shivering on the hillsides, the lowly and despised, not the powerful and the comfortable, were the ones chosen for the greatest theophany of all time.

The significance of what happened to the shepherds can be summed up in one word: *dignity*. We are reminded that those who were once despised possess an inherent dignity before God. Though unwelcome in the palaces of the privileged, they were welcomed by God as worthy to receive the good news. In the long history of salvation, the Augustuses and the Quiriniuses would have only *apparent* power; *real* power would now reside in those chosen by God to receive the good news. *That's* dignity.

And so we have in Luke a kind of gospel within the Gospel. It is the gospel according to the shepherds. Its theme is dignity. Its action is short but revealing. The gospel proclaimed by the shepherds to the tiny church at Bethlehem is this: God has deposed the mighty; God has raised up the lowly.

We *must* hear the shepherds' gospel if we want to appreciate fully what happened when Jesus was born. We regard that moment as a critical point in human history, for that is when God chose the ordinary to witness something extraordinary. God chose those who seemed to not have dignity to share in the dignity of the incarnation. The shepherds echo and embody Mary's own words at the annunciation—The Lord, the Mighty One, has done great things for me. He has lifted up the lowly.

If we listen carefully down through the centuries, we hear the shepherds' gospel again and again. It is heard centuries later, in a land far distant from Bethlehem. The story begins in 1530, in what would come to be known as Mexico. A man, as lowly as the shepherds, Juan Diego by name, is making his way to Tlatelolco to attend Mass and receive catechetical instruction.[4] At a hill named Tepeyac, he has a strange encounter. A young woman, a woman more beautiful than anyone he had seen before, stops him. She reveals that she is the Virgin Mary, and she has a special request for him: He must ask the bishop to build a temple there on Tepeyac Hill.

You know this story. It is the story of St. Juan Diego and the Virgin of Guadalupe, a feast we celebrated just a few weeks ago on December 12. As the story goes, Juan Diego tries to evade the Virgin's request. He protests that he is unworthy and incapable of convincing the bishop. But Mary addresses Juan Diego as "the dearest of my children" and orders him to try again. Eventually, Juan Diego succeeds. He fills his tilma with roses, miraculously blooming in winter, and carries them to the bishop. When he unfolds the garment, the roses drop to the floor and a beautiful image of the Virgin appears on his garment.

One word describes that encounter between Juan Diego and the Virgin—*dignity*. When he first meets the Virgin, Juan Diego is a shy, self-effacing peasant. He speaks of himself as a piece of dirt. But as his encounter with the Virgin continues, he changes. He becomes a man aware of his own dignity, even to the point of being able to speak boldly to the Virgin and to carry out her instructions.

The encounter with the Virgin of Guadalupe gave new dignity to Juan Diego and to all the indigenous people struggling under the oppression of Spain. Aware of their own dignity, the Mexican people would establish their own culture, their own identity, their own country. We in this country are enriched by the gifts of the people of Mexico who in their celebration of the Virgin of Guadalupe celebrate their own dignity.

Our tradition is filled with accounts of the children of God realizing their dignity. Throughout his ministry, Jesus repeatedly embraced those who lacked dignity—lepers, prostitutes, sinners. The theme of dignity, which the shepherds first proclaimed, is unavoidable in the Gospel. We rejoice as well with the shepherds this morning, for we know that our dignity as persons made in the image and likeness of God has been established as the central message of Christmas. We need only to claim it and proclaim it—God has raised up the lowly. That is the shepherds' gospel.

Questions for Further Discussion:

1. How might a shepherds' gospel be different from the ones we have?

2. Are you familiar with the story of Our Lady of Guadalupe? What does it say about the dignity of all people?

9

SING JOYFULLY TO A HOMELESS GOD
Christmas Day (A)

- Isaiah 52:7–10
- Hebrews 1:1–6
- John 1:1–18

Imagine the Lord, for the first time, from darkness, and stranded
Immensely in distance, recognizing Himself in the Son Of Man:
His homelessness plain to him now in a homeless one.
                              "Nativity Poem," by Joseph Brodsky[5]

On this day, Christmas Day, we celebrate with joy that moment in time when God became homeless!

At first, it may strike us as inappropriate to be joyful at the thought of God becoming homeless. But we are talking here about a different kind of homelessness; not the homelessness of the many people who pass through our local St. Anne's Shelter, and whose lives are anything but joyful. No, the homelessness of God is more like a divine pilgrimage, a mission undertaken by God not to wander aimlessly in the world but to accept homelessness for a very specific goal— *to find a home in the heart of each one of us.* That is what gives us joy this day: that God would undergo a voluntary homelessness in order to make it possible for us to return to our true home.

If you were at Mass this morning, or last night at midnight, you would have heard the story of a homeless family. Mary and Joseph left their home in Nazareth, traveled all the way to Bethlehem without reservations for a place to stay. They were homeless, until they found their way to a rough stable, or cave, a kind of first-century homeless shelter. In a few short days, Scripture tells us, they would be homeless again, fleeing into Egypt to escape the murderous intent of Herod.

But the homelessness of God that the poet, Joseph Brodsky, had in mind in the lines quoted at the outset goes beyond the plight of the homeless Holy Family. The poet echoes the words of the prologue to John's Gospel, which we just heard read. In this beautiful Johannine hymn, which for centuries was used as a blessing in Catholic liturgical tradition,[6] the author traces the roots of Jesus, not to his birth at Bethlehem or his conception at Nazareth, but to the very beginning. The author uses the exact same words that are used to begin the book of Genesis, "In the beginning…." He identifies Jesus as the Word that was with God before creation. And even though all creation came into being through him, when he came to what was his own, "his own people did not accept him" (John 1:11). The Word was, in a word, *homeless*.

Why did God become homeless? To share in the poverty of our human condition and thereby make it possible for us to return to our true home. Incredible as it may seem, the Word willingly, and joyfully, sought out our weakness, knowing that weakness would be transformed into the great power of love—the power of the resurrection. The path of weakness and vulnerability that starts with the incarnation leads directly to the cross and resurrection.

God became homeless, but not for long. To those who would accept him, who would give him a home in their hearts, "he gave power to become children of God" (John 1:12). The prologue we just heard is like an overture for a great musical composition. It gives us a hint of what we will hear in the remainder of the Gospel. In the first twelve chapters of John, the Gospel will show how Jesus came to his own with the words of eternal life, but was rejected. The final chapters—thirteen through twenty—show how the gift of life was given to those who did accept him. That choice continues in our day. The words are still spoken, signs still given, but not all accept him. You are here today because you do accept him. You must deepen that acceptance, make it more unconditional, more aware, during every moment of your life.

The joy of this day is that the God who became homeless has found a home in us. We are the tent in which the glory of God now resides. Christ seeks a home in the simplicity of the human heart. These words are like the beautiful feet of a messenger upon the mountains "who brings glad tidings, announcing peace, bearing good news, announcing salvation" (Isa 52:7).

By coming among us as the homeless one, God awakens in us a deep memory of our true home. We see in the innocence of a child in a manger a reminder of our own innocence when, before our relationship was disrupted, we were at home with God. Our worship of God in the form of the Christ Child enlivens our desire to continue the journey to the home from whence we came.

How, then, do we make that journey? We do it by welcoming the Word into the homes of our hearts. Certainly, we do so by gathering as we have this day in prayer, in worship, in celebrating Eucharist. But, of course, it does not end here. We are sent out to enter into closer relationship with those who are weak. That is why the homeless must be treated with hospitality, for they are the living reminders of the weakness and vulnerability of God, a God who became homeless for us. When we care for the homeless, we receive back from them, if we are open to receive it, the gift of a deeper awareness of our own weakness. And when we bring that weakness to God, it is transformed into love. God does not want our strength as much as our weakness. It is our weakness as humility, as total dependence on God, that has the potential of being transformed into our greatest strength. It is that strength, a God-transformed strength, that enables us to care for the homeless in this life and to journey with them to our true home in the heart of God.

Questions for Further Discussion:

1. Have you ever thought of God as being homeless? Why would God become homeless?

2. What does it mean to receive from the homeless the gift of a deeper awareness of our own weakness? Why does God want our weakness more than our strength?

10
THE CROSS AT BETHLEHEM
Holy Family (A)

- Sirach 3:2–6, 12–14
- Colossians 3:12–21
- Matthew 2:13–15, 19–23

In his controversial movie, *The Passion of the Christ,* Mel Gibson dramatizes the events of Jesus' agony during the crucifixion, including a scene where Jesus stumbles and helplessly falls to the ground. Mary, who is following the struggles of her son on the road to Calvary, is horrified. As she stares in anguish at her son sprawled in the dust, her memory flashes back to a scene from Jesus' childhood. She recalls how the boy Jesus fell while playing and how she ran to him, how she comforted and consoled him. The scene is startling and effective, because it reminds us that Jesus did not just appear on the scene as an adult. He had a childhood. And that childhood, too, adds an important dimension to the gospel message of God's Son coming into the world to suffer and die on the cross.

Matthew may have had this thought in mind when he included in his Gospel the story we just heard. The flight into Egypt and the return to Nazareth mark the end of Matthew's infancy narrative. After today's account, Matthew leaps forward in time to the start of Jesus' public ministry, starting with his baptism by John the Baptist. The drama that builds as Jesus confronts hostile Jewish authorities reaches a crescendo at Calvary. The cross is the central symbol of the passion narrative. And yet, if we are attentive, we see how the infancy narrative as well contains subtle but real connections to the suffering, death, and resurrection of Jesus. The shadow of the cross is present, even at Bethlehem.

The Gospel we just heard shows that from his earliest days Jesus attracted the hostility of the powerful who feared losing power. An angel warns Joseph in a dream that Herod intends to search for the child and destroy him. Scholars tell us that the Greek verb for *destroy, apollynai,* which Matthew uses to express the angel's warning to Joseph, "Herod is going to search for the child to destroy him..." (Matt 2:13), is the same verb used in the passion narrative to describe how the priests and elders wished to destroy Jesus (Matt 27:20).[7] Matthew seems to be telling us that at both the beginning and end of his life Jesus was vulnerable. The forces that would demand his life in the praetorium at Jerusalem were also conspiring to take his life in the stable at Bethlehem. The familiar and warm images of the baby Jesus in a manger surrounded by shepherds and magi cannot entirely obscure the reality of the cross that will follow him throughout his life.

But like the passion narrative that would come much later in Matthew's Gospel, the infancy narrative reveals another more powerful force at work in the unfolding drama. Just as God did not abandon Jesus at Calvary, so too God would act to save the child Jesus, warning him through the mediation of an angel and protecting him through the courage and skill of his foster father, Joseph. Through the use of the long genealogy of Jesus, Matthew shows us that Jesus was truly the son of

David, son of Abraham. Today's account assures us that God would not allow the promise of a savior to be thwarted by any worldly force.

If the cross followed Jesus throughout *his* childhood, then we should not be surprised that the cross is present in the lives or our own children as well. Millions of children today, both the born and the unborn, are vulnerable to powerful forces beyond their control. Now it is not the hostility of Herod that haunts the smallest representatives of Christ; it is, instead, the scourge of being unwanted, the evil of hunger and disease, the forces of war and dislocation that stalk the most vulnerable among us. The cross that casts its shadow over the children of our world today is the same cross that followed Jesus from Bethlehem to Calvary.

We cannot know with much certainty any of the details of Jesus' early life. But this we can know with certainty: Jesus was vulnerable before the forces of his day. But from the very beginning to the very end Jesus would know the loving protection of his Father, manifested in the care and protection of his foster father, Joseph, and his mother, Mary. We now stand in the place of Joseph and Mary, protecting, nurturing, and caring for the children who stand in the place of the child Jesus.

Questions for Further Discussion:

1. In what ways do you see children today vulnerable to hostile forces as Jesus was?

2. What can we as a community do to protect them?

11
WHAT IS A GOSPEL?
Solemnity of Mary, the Mother of God (A)

> • Numbers 6:22–27
> • Galatians 4:4–7
> • Luke 2:16–21

In his book, *Reading the Gospels with the Church,* Father Raymond E. Brown notes, "I have often thought that in January, as we begin in parishes to read the Gospel for the Sundays of a new year (Matthew for Year A; Mark for Year B; Luke for Year C), it would be helpful for priests to devote a homily to what a Gospel is, and another homily to what is special about the Gospel that will be read all year long."[8] This being the first day of January, it seemed like the perfect time to follow Father Brown's advice. Let me, then, say a few words about what a gospel is and, then, how that understanding can help us find meaning in today's readings.

Father Brown reminds us that the gospels were *not* intended to be biographies of Jesus. To allay any fears that may arise from learning that the gospels are not literal accounts of Jesus' ministry, he points us to the official teaching of the Catholic Church found in an *Instruction* on "The Historical Truth of the Gospels," issued by the Roman Pontifical Biblical Commission in 1964, which would later form the substance of Vatican II's *Constitution on Divine Revelation.*[9]

The *Instruction* points out that each of the gospels was the end product of three distinct stages of tradition. The first stage is the public ministry of Jesus of Nazareth. During this stage, which occurred during the first third of the first century, Jesus taught and ministered in Galilee. Those who heard his teaching and witnessed his signs and miracles quite naturally chose to present to their listeners those parts of Jesus' message they deemed most pertinent. They would have preserved those aspects of Jesus' teaching that bore upon the relevant issues of their time, just as we do today.

The second stage of gospel development concerns the apostolic preaching about Jesus, which probably extended through the second third of the first century. What the apostles had seen and heard was now filtered through their own faith experience. In the light of the resurrection, they preached the truth of Jesus in a way that was interpretive and committed. As the early Church spread into foreign lands, preachers were forced to translate the message of Jesus into new languages and utilize new modes of expression. The preaching to urban Jewish converts would be considerably different from that heard by Greek Gentiles. In sum, the preaching demanded during the apostolic age was a living, meaningful presentation of the message of Jesus in ways that would appeal to diverse audiences. While it was faithful to what Jesus said, it was *not* a literal reproduction of the events of Jesus' life.

The third stage of development was the actual writing of the gospels, which probably happened during the final third of the first century. Again, the writing process was a selective one. The *Instruction* says, "From the many things handed down they selected some things, reduced others to a synthesis, [still] others they explicated as they kept in mind the situation of the Churches."[10] The "situation of the

Churches" for which the gospels were written determined the sequence of events related, the words chosen, and the context in which they were placed. The *Instruction* concludes, *"[T]he doctrine and life of Jesus were not simply reported for the sole purpose of being remembered, but were 'preached' so as to offer the Church a basis of faith and morals."*[1] [emphasis in the original]

The light given us by our Church through the insights of biblical scholars like the late Father Raymond Brown, as well as through official teaching expressed in a document like the *Instruction,* enables us to approach the infancy narratives we have heard during the Christmas season in a truly Catholic way. We need not insist on a literal interpretation of the infancy narratives; equally important, we do not regard them as simply mythical accounts. We believe that through the guidance of the Holy Spirit, the gospels give us the truth about Jesus we need to know. What, then, do we need to know from today's Gospel?

We need to know that the ancient blessing of God given to Aaron through Moses has been fulfilled. God has blessed not only the Israelites with graciousness and peace but all people. God blessed the world, as Paul says to the Galatians, by sending his Son, "born of a woman, born under the law, to ransom those under the law, so that we might receive adoption as sons" (Gal 4:4–5). That is what the apostles preached; that is what the authors of the gospels recorded.

But, you ask, "What about the shepherds? Were they there, as Luke records?" We have no way of knowing for sure. What we *do* know from those who wrote the gospels is that Jesus was not recognized as Lord by everyone, especially not by those in positions of power and prestige. On the other hand, he was recognized consistently by the poor and the powerless. Why shepherds, then? Because at the time of Jesus' birth, they were part of the lowest social class. By the time Luke wrote his Gospel, it was well established that Jesus had been most easily recognized by the poor, by women, by outcasts of every sort. Luke weaves that thread of recognition all the way through his Gospel, starting with the shepherds.

Finally, there is Mary. On this feast of Mary, the Mother of God, she may give us the best image for understanding what a gospel is. Luke says that she "kept all these things, reflecting on them in her heart" (Luke 2:19). Like Mary, we are invited during this coming year to gather up all the details we can about the life of Jesus but, more importantly, to ponder these words in our hearts. From that reflection, guided by the Holy Spirit in the Church, we come to know even better the message Jesus left us in the gospels.

Questions for Further Discussion:

1. Can you summarize the three stages of gospel formation? How might the words we read today have been shaped by the process of gospel formation?

2. What do you feel we need to know from today's Gospel?

12
MAY I HOLD THE BABY?
Epiphany of the Lord

- Isaiah 60:1–6
- Ephesians 3:2–3a, 5–6
- Matthew 2:1–12

Our manger scene is now complete. When light flooded the darkness Christmas morning, we rejoiced at the appearance of Mary, Joseph, and the child Jesus. Shepherds crowded in around the Holy Family, while angels rejoiced in the heavens. Today, on this feast of Epiphany, we welcome the last to arrive—magi, three kings of the Orient, wise men who came to adore the divine, now miraculously united with the human.

What do we see in these strange worshipers, these amiable ambassadors from the pagan world, mysteriously guided to this moment of epiphany when the incarnation was manifested to the world? Are they simply pious posers for Christmas cards? Are they merely figurines that collect dust in the church basement, until Advent briefly liberates them?

After Mass last night, a woman came up to me and asked, "Do you know how we know they were wise men and not wise women?"

"No," I said, "Tell me."

"Well," she said, "if they had been women, they would have asked for directions and gotten to Bethlehem on time; they would have brought a casserole, made clothes for the baby, cleaned up the place, and...there would be peace on earth!"

I said I thought that sounded like feminist theology, but I would try to work it in.

Indeed, the wise men, or wise women, are much more than pious posers or pretty figurines, for they represent the first manifestation of

Christ to the world. More than that, they symbolize the journey each one of us makes through life in our search for God. Finally, if you permit a little poetic license, they point to our own Eucharist.

About the wise men, we know virtually nothing. No provable facts, only legends have come down to us. We know nothing of what they believed in, nothing of their practices; we cannot say for sure what became of them. We know only that they followed a star, seeking the infinite now manifested in the finite. And that is what we do too, for at the ground of our being, in the depths of our hearts, that still point in our soul that is as secret as the lives of the three wise men, we discover something we share with these ancient pilgrims: an insatiable longing for God.

People know us by our personalities, our accomplishments perhaps, our good deeds, as well as our foibles. But only God knows us at the deepest level of our lives. At that level, we find what we have in common with the wise men: a God-given desire to seek the infinite wherever it is manifested in the finite. That is what brought the wise men across ancient deserts; that is what brings us here this morning.

But now it is not an infant in a manger; now it is the Bread of Life, the Eucharist, that draws us to this church. Like the wise men, each of us has followed a star, not a star in the heavens but a star of faith that has guided us through times clouded by doubt, perhaps times of despairing darkness, until we arrive once again to experience the divine manifested in the material, the uncreated in the created, Christ present in bread and wine.

The figurines depict the wise men as kneeling or standing in rapt adoration. And this is a correct image, for they were present at a great mystery. St. Gregory Nazianzen says that in the presence of mystery, adoration, not inquiry, is the appropriate response. And they adored, just as we adore the infinite manifested in the finite every time we come to Mass.

But I have to believe there is more to this scene. I think that if I were an artist, I would depict one of the wise men doing something very human. I would portray him cradling the baby Jesus in his arms. I would do this because, while adoration is appropriate, we also have a human impulse to touch, to hold, to taste the divine, present in the ordinary stuff of life.

And so, I easily picture the scene this way: One of the ancient pilgrims, his face radiating the joy of adoration, comes timidly forward and says to Mary, "May I hold the baby?" And Mary, good Jewish mother that she was, gently places the baby in the old man's arms. Adoration has led him to the most exquisite human contact imaginable—to hold the divine in human hands!

Does this scene not also suggest to us our eucharistic celebration? We adore Christ present in our assembly, in the word of God proclaimed, in the priest at the altar, in the consecrated bread and wine, but there comes a moment when we imitate what the wise men must have done. We come forward to receive Christ, with one hand cradling the other, slightly elevated, a human throne on which to place the infinite now manifested in finite bread. And the Church, through her ministers, responds like Mary, carefully placing the divine in our hands.

But even as they were adoring and holding the Christ, there was in the minds of the wise men an ominous thought. It was the dream. The dream had warned them that this child lived with danger. The dream hints of a life of suffering, of blood to be shed, and of death. So too, when we turn to the cup we are reminded that this Christ Child will grow to become a man and will shed his blood on Good Friday.

The wise men came, they adored, and they left. But they must have left as changed men. They went back to their worlds, just as we do at the end of Mass, as changed people sent out to change the world. We can say this, because we have seen it happen in other wise men and women, even in our own times. Archbishop Romero, who died a martyr's death in El Salvador, traveled the same path as the wise men, the same path we travel. He too adored Christ and held Christ in his hands many times. The experience changed him, for on December 24, 1979, he spoke these words in a sermon to his people: "We must not seek the child Jesus in the pretty figurines of our Christmas cribs. We must seek Him among the undernourished children who have gone to bed tonight with nothing to eat."[12]

With the Christmas season now complete, the wise men and the other figurines can be returned to their dusty cells. But they will have served their purpose only if we leave this season with renewed zeal to care for those in need, especially the children. Like the wise men, our worship, our adoration must prompt us to ask: "May I hold the baby?"

"May I hold the Iraqi baby who, as a result of our actions, has suffered the ravages of war?"

"May I hold the African baby orphaned by AIDS?"

"May I hold the immigrant baby, the welfare baby, here in our own community, so often in need of caring hands?"

If we follow the wise men, we will continually ask these questions. The answers we give will affect our world.

Questions for Further Discussion:

1. Do you see an image of the Eucharist in the visit of the wise men?

2. Where are the babies that wise men and women today must ask to hold?

13
FAITH ENGAGING CULTURE
Baptism of the Lord (A)

- Isaiah 42:1–4, 6–7
- Acts 10:34–38
- Matthew 3:13–17

Some of us may remember the TV series *Mission Impossible,* which began with the line, "Your mission, if you choose to accept it, is...." Then would follow a description of a seemingly impossible mission, which would inevitably be accepted.

That is, in part, what today's readings are about—*mission.* The Baptism of the Lord is, in one sense, a continuation of the feast of Epiphany, for we again have a manifestation of Christ to the world. Matthew records that after Jesus was baptized, a voice came from the heavens saying, "This is my beloved Son, with whom I am well pleased" (Matt 3:17). The voice from the heavens is directed not to Jesus alone but to the world. It announces that the servant, spoken of by Isaiah in the first reading, the chosen one with whom God is pleased, is this Jesus who will be manifested to the entire world. The ongoing manifestation of the good news, that God is among us, then becomes the mission of Jesus, the mission of the Church, and our mission.

In the second reading, we have a wonderful example of how that mission was carried out in the early Church. The story of Peter and Cornelius recorded in Acts shows us that the mission of the Church can be described as faith engaging culture. In Acts, it is the faith of Peter that engages the culture of a Roman world.

To understand the significance of the story in Acts you have to go back to the start of the chapter. If you want to fully appreciate this story, I urge you this afternoon to sit down and read all of Acts, chapter 10. It is a fascinating story illustrating how faith engages culture.

Cornelius was a product of Roman culture, the head of a Roman army cohort at Caesarea, but a man who is also described as "a devout man who feared God" (Acts 10:2 NRSV). In a vision, he is told to send for Peter, who is staying nearby in Joppa. He sends messengers who arrive at Peter's residence at about the same time that Peter has received a vision clarifying for him that everything created by God is pure, not unclean as he was accustomed to believe. At the behest of the messengers, Peter travels to Caesarea and is greeted by Cornelius. Then, Peter, still thinking of himself as a Jew, says to Cornelius, "You yourselves know that it is unlawful for a Jew to associate with or to visit a Gentile; but God has shown me that I should not call anyone profane or unclean" (Acts 10:28 NRSV). Then follows the address we hear in the second reading where Peter declares: "In truth, I see that God shows no partiality. Rather, in every nation whoever fears him and acts uprightly is acceptable to him" (Acts 10:34). Peter's faith had engaged Roman culture, and the world would never be the same again. The Greco-Roman world was soon to become a mission field for the followers of Christ.

The great theologian, Karl Rahner, identified three great epochs in Church history:

> First, the short period of Jewish Christianity. Second, the period of the Church in a distinct cultural region, namely, that of [Greek and European culture and civilization]. Third, the period in which the sphere of the Church's life is in fact the entire world.[13]

The story of Cornelius and Peter is from the first period. The second period probably reaches to modern times and Vatican II. The third period we are living in right now. And once again we see the ongoing mission of the Church as faith engaging culture. There can be no better example of that principle than the Servant of God John Paul II—John Paul the Great—the pope who traveled millions of miles and visited hundreds of countries in his twenty-six-plus-year-pontificate. John Paul II, the spiritual descendant of Peter, demonstrated, probably better than any pope of the twentieth century, how faith can engage cultures all over the globe. A good example was the pope's visit to Cuba in the 1990s. There, John Paul II directly engaged a culture shaped by the modern ideology of Marxism. In his visit to Cuba, it was clear that John Paul II was carrying out that great mission of manifesting God's presence in the world, a mission that began with Jesus the moment he stepped out of the Jordan River some two-thousand years ago.

But, of course, the mission of faith engaging culture is not restricted to popes. Each of us is engaged in that same mission every day. We all live, work, and recreate in a culture. And our mission as Catholics in the twenty-first century is to engage that culture with the same joy and vigor demonstrated by Peter two-thousand years ago, by John Paul II in our own time, and his successor, Benedict XVI, the self-described "gentle, humble servant."

To effectively engage the culture of America in this new millennium, two things are necessary: first, an intelligent understanding of our culture—what it is, and how it differs from the Christian culture envisioned by John Paul II. It is as wrong to think that *everything* about our culture is bad as it is to uncritically embrace it. The obligation of Catholics is to be intelligent and loving critics of our culture.

Second, we must have a vigorous faith if we are to effectively criticize and challenge a culture that differs in so many ways from what we envision as a Catholic-Christian culture. This is no small task. It is a life-long process. And it begins with our children. In our Catholic schools, and in our religious-education programs, we begin the development of skills for questioning, critiquing, and challenging culture. It is there that we begin to learn what is art and what is merely a cheap imitation of art; there we learn to distinguish between useful information and what is actually propaganda; there we begin to experience the difference between a life shaped by gospel values and a life based on the shifting sands of pop culture.

We are fortunate to have in our parish a Catholic elementary school and a high school where young people can gain the faith that will be needed to effectively engage the culture of the twenty-first century. The real hope of transforming our culture and carrying on the mission of Christ lies with these young people.

We are indeed on a mission to the entire world. It is a glorious mission, stretching back two millennia and extending indefinitely into the future. It can be our mission, if we choose to accept it.

Questions for Further Discussion:

1. Where do you see faith engaging culture today?
2. How can you be better equipped in terms of your faith to engage the culture of our times?

PART THREE
Ordinary Time
HOMILIES 14–17

[W]e are not confined to gospel images. The good news of the
kingdom is a living, developing reality. Each generation of disciples
finds new ways to interpret and apply the teachings of Christ to its
own experience. Today Christ still speaks powerfully through
scriptural images, but he can also teach us through images drawn
from our daily lives: construction sites, silverware,
fictional characters, and park benches, among others.

Archbishop George H. Niederauer,
Precious as Silver: Imagining Your Life with God[1]

14

KEEPING A PROPER PERSPECTIVE ON THE NEWS
Second Sunday in Ordinary Time (A)

- Isaiah 49:3, 5–6
- 1 Corinthians 1:1–3
- John 1:29–34

A recent letter to the editor of our local Catholic paper, *Intermountain Catholic,* expressed "profound disappointment and chagrin" over a headline that appeared at the end of 2002 announcing, "Clergy sex abuse was biggest religious news of the year."[2] The writer goes on to point out the many other noteworthy events that had happened, including the canonization of men and women in our own hemisphere during the year just ended. The writer urged the paper to not go the way of the "scandal mongering secular press" by publishing only the negative while burying the positive in the less conspicuous pages.

My purpose here is not to argue with the points made by the writer but, instead, to simply suggest that we take the long view of events, news events, world events, and especially the reporting of events. The "good news" is never quite clear to those who are immediately exposed to events. It takes time and, I would suggest, the help of the Holy Spirit over time, to separate what is good news from what is bad.

If you were the publisher of a Catholic newspaper sometime around AD 28 and were following the events that are the basis for the Gospel reading we just heard, you might come out with a headline that read: "John Witnesses to Jesus as Son of God." Now that's good news! But as Bible scholars and historians have dug back into the historical events that underlie what we just heard, they have discovered a lot of bad news as well. They have discovered scandal, separation, division and discord, none of which appears in the Gospel under a headline.[3] And yet, our trusted Catholic scholars argue convincingly that it was there.

Let us start with John the Baptist himself. First of all, notice that today's Gospel does not refer to him as "the Baptist" unlike the synoptic gospels—Matthew, Mark, and Luke—who picture John baptizing Jesus. One scholar describes the John mentioned in today's reading as the "un-Baptist,"[4] a strange figure who did not fit easily into the

Christian view of things. The reason he appears today as the "un-Baptist" is because of other headlines that our fictitious Catholic publisher used but which never survived the revisionist publishers who came later. Some of these headlines read, "Jesus Submits to Baptism by John," "Jesus Becomes a Follower of John the Baptist," "Followers of John Join Jesus," "Jesus Begins Own Baptismal Ministry," and finally, "Baptist Sectarians Leave Johannine Community." Behind each of these headlines lies a story of ordinary humans, struggling just as we do to discern the truth in the midst of a swirl of events.

What a scandal it must have been for the first-century followers of Jesus to confront the fact that Jesus had undergone baptism by John, that Jesus was likely a follower of John for a while, and that Jesus imitated John for a time in a baptismal ministry. And finally, the headlines point to a now-lost story of human weakness, of our human tendency to divide up our loyalties, and, when the tension strains relationships too far, of our tendency to split into rival camps. *I* am a follower of *Jesus; you* are a follower of John the *Baptist*.

The fictitious headlines I just gave you did not survive, because the author of John's Gospel, like the authors of the other gospels, was not interested in presenting a blow-by-blow account of how the early Church evolved. The author of John's Gospel was not oblivious to troublesome facts, but, as we believe, under the guidance of the Holy Spirit, he gave us what is essential for us to know: that there was a man named John who was the first witness to the great truth that Jesus came from God. Thus, the only headline that remains relevant for our own spiritual well-being is what we just heard—"John Witnesses to Jesus as Son of God."

How then does this understanding of the events leading up to this morning's Gospel help us in these early days of the twenty-first century? I would suggest that they remind us of the importance of perspective and patience. Perspective is what the writer to *Intermountain Catholic* was arguing for, and rightfully so. We are barraged by news these days, but, in truth, there is little that is new under the sun. The headlines that appeared from AD 28 when John the Baptist walked onto the stage of history until the first publication of today's Gospel record only the most obvious developments of the time. Underneath the radar screen of public notice, tiny, graced actions were occurring that were of much greater significance. The truth that Jesus is, indeed, the Son of God would not become clear to many until much later, and would not be officially stated as Church dogma for centuries. In the meantime, those who witnessed to this obscure truth, like John the

Baptist, would cling to it, even die for it, just as did the "wonderful men and women canonized in our hemisphere this year." The sifting and sorting of history that gives us the perspective we need is a slow, arduous process, but the result is a life-giving product: knowledge of the truth necessary for our salvation.

And so, we must learn patience in approaching the news. John the Baptist's words witnessing to Jesus as the Son of God were probably spoken between AD 28 and April 7, AD 30,[5] when one scholar says Jesus died on the cross. The words were probably not recorded in John's Gospel until around AD 90. *Sixty years passed* before the early Church knew what the biggest religious news of the early years was.

We might ask ourselves: Sixty years from now, what will be the headline of this past year that survives?

One hint: It will be shaped by the Holy Spirit and it will say something about Jesus Christ at work in his Church.

Questions for Further Discussion:

1. Do you find the reporting of religious news to be "fair and balanced"? Are you able to approach the news with patience and perspective?

2. If you were writing a newspaper headline concerning the Catholic Church sixty years from now, what do you think it would be?

15

VOCATION: FALLING IN LOVE WITH GOD
Third Sunday in Ordinary Time (A)

- Isaiah 8:23—9:3
- 1 Corinthians 1:10–13, 17
- Matthew 4:12–23

There is a marvelous urgency in today's Gospel scene. Jesus appears on the shore and says, "Come after me," and immediately Simon and Andrew abandon their nets and follow him. Jesus walks a little farther, and sees James and John mending their nets. He calls. Immediately, they leave their father in the boat and scramble after him.

What a marvelous vocations director Jesus was! He did not invite young men to a period of discernment. He did not outline a course of study. He did not even mention what this new life would be like. Just, "Come...follow me." And they came.

This familiar Gospel scene begs the question: *Why?* Why did these grown men act like children following the Pied Piper? Where do we go to find something that will help us understand the call of Jesus and its effect on these men?

Certainly, there are many ways of accounting for the disciples' behavior, but I want to suggest a *love* story as the key to understanding what happened that morning on the Sea of Galilee. I am going to tell you a love story, because responding to the call of the Lord, whether it be in the first century or the twenty-first, is all about loving God more than fishing nets, more than father and friends; indeed, it is about loving God more than anything in the world.

Here is the love story. It is from the Sufi tradition and involves the great poet, Hafiz.[6] Since Hafiz lived in the fourteenth century, it may be as much legend as fact. No matter. It's a wonderful love story.

Hafiz was a poor baker's assistant in the town of Shiraz in modern-day Iran. As part of his job, Hafiz delivered bread to a mansion where one day he caught a fleeting glimpse of a beautiful young woman on the terrace. Hafiz fell madly in love with her but she never even noticed him. She was from a wealthy noble family and he was a poor baker's assistant. She was beautiful, he was short and physically unattractive— the situation was hopeless.

As the months went by, Hafiz composed poems and love songs about this beautiful woman, celebrating her beauty and his great longing for her. People would hear Hafiz singing his poems and they would repeat them; his poems became popular all over Shiraz.

Hafiz thought only of his beloved. So desperate was he that one day he decided to undertake an arduous spiritual discipline that required him to keep vigil at the tomb of a certain saint all night long for forty nights. It was said that anyone who could accomplish this near impossible austerity would be granted his heart's desire.

Every day Hafiz went to work at the bakery; every night he forced himself to stay awake for love of this beautiful girl. His love was so strong that he succeeded in completing this vigil.

At daybreak on the fortieth day, the archangel Gabriel appeared before Hafiz and told him to ask for whatever he wished. Hafiz had never seen such a glorious, radiant being as Gabriel. He found himself thinking, "If God's messenger is so beautiful, how much more beautiful must God be." Gazing on the unimaginable splendor of God's angel, Hafiz forgot all about the girl, he forgot about his wish, he forgot everything. He said simply, "I want God!"

And so Gabriel directed him to a spiritual teacher who lived in Shiraz. The angel told Hafiz to serve this teacher in every way and his wish would be fulfilled. And so he did.

Today we have the poems of Hafiz that are some of the most beautiful expressions of one man's love affair with God. They are ecstatic poetry, poetry filled with the delight and joy of someone who has chosen God over all else. One translator of Hafiz says that his poetry "can be read as a record of a human being's journey to perfect joy, perfect knowing, and perfect love."[7]

And isn't that what the call of Simon and Andrew, James and John was all about? A journey to perfect joy, knowing and love. And they responded as they did because, like Hafiz, they had seen someone more beautiful, more attractive, than anything they had loved up until then.

The ancient writers of our tradition say that angels appear as radiant, glorious beings because they are veiling the glory of God. They shield us from the face of God, which no one can see and still live. Christ, too, veiled the glory of God. By becoming incarnate, God accommodated the great beauty, the glory of God, for our human eyes. But even veiled, what the disciples saw was enough to cause them to say with their feet what Hafiz expressed in words, "I want God."

A vocation is captured simply in those words, "I want God." Only the direct knowledge of a God more beautiful than any human experience can trigger the kind of urgent response we find in today's Gospel.

But there is something else involved: There is the long, patient waiting at the tomb of the saint. It is only after the long and arduous spiritual journey that the theophany occurs. In other words, there is discipline involved, sacrifice, there is an ascetic life that frees one from all the wants, all the cares, that keep Christ from breaking through to us. Hafiz gave up the comfort of sleep. While I would not suggest such a thing to sleep-deprived Americans, perhaps there is some other more significant comfort each of us must leave behind. Perhaps it is the comfort of an affluent lifestyle, or maybe just the comfort we sometimes take in judging others. Envy, jealousy, the many petty indulgences we allow ourselves may well be the comfort we must leave behind in our vigil.

In closing, let me leave you with just a couple lines from Hafiz. He says in one of his poems, "I am a hole in a flute that the Christ's breath moves through. Listen to this music."

Each of us is called by Christ, just as surely as were the disciples, to become a perfect hole in the flute through which Christ's breath moves. That is what we are about in this Eucharist and that is what our lives are about when we leave here—we live so as to become unique parts of a finely crafted instrument played by the Divine Musician. Through the lives we live as followers of Christ we say to the world— Listen to this music!

Questions for Further Discussion:

1. Does the idea of vocation as falling in love with God appeal to you? Why or why not?
2. What does it mean to be "a hole in a flute that the Christ breath moves through?"

16
CLIMBING MT. BEATITUDE
Fourth Sunday in Ordinary Time (A)

- Zephaniah 2:3; 3:12–13
- 1 Corinthians 1:26–31
- Matthew 5:1–12a

On May 29, 1953, at 11:30 a.m., Sir Edmund Hillary and his Sherpa guide, Tensing Norgay, became the first humans to reach Earth's highest point—the summit of Mt. Everest in the Himalayas. The accomplishment stands as one of the high points of human physical endurance. Hillary would later be knighted and lead other exploratory expeditions to the South Pole and the source of the Yangtze River.

But it is scaling the highest mountain in the world that will always be Hillary's great claim to fame. Mountain peaks, seemingly inaccessible to mere mortals, have always had a kind of religious mystique about them. I suspect that when the first of our ancestors stepped out onto the plains of Africa and gazed up at a towering peak, there was a sense of religious awe, together with a desire to go there. One of my favorite pictures in the collection of black-and-white photographs at the Trappist monastery in Huntsville, Utah, is one of a group of monks, noticeably younger than today, standing on the top of Mt. Ogden, Utah, looking every bit as triumphant as Sir Edmund Hillary. A peak experience in the Trappist tradition.

Mountains have great religious significance in the drama of salvation history played out in both the Old and New Testaments. After surviving the great flood, Noah's ark came to rest on the mountains of Ararat (Genesis 7:4); at Mt. Horeb, "the mountain of God," an angel of the Lord first appeared to Moses in a burning bush and mediated God's command to lead the people of Israel out of Egypt (Exodus 3); it was on Mt. Sinai that Moses would receive the Ten Commandments (Exodus 19); Elijah was commanded to "[g]o out and stand on the mountain before the LORD, for the LORD is about to pass by" (1 Kgs 19:11 NRSV); and when Jesus was tempted in the desert, Matthew says, "[T]he devil took him to a very high mountain" (Matt 4:8 NRSV). When it comes to events of religious significance, mountains have long been a favorite venue.

In today's Gospel, God is encountered on still another mountain. It is fitting that a mountain would be the place where Jesus would share with his disciples a sermon that can be described in two ways: (1) a character sketch of Jesus and (2) a map to show us how to reach the heights of the spiritual life. If we can follow that map faithfully, we may expect to find true happiness.

The *Catechism of the Catholic Church* says that "the Beatitudes respond to the natural desire for happiness." It is a desire "of divine origin: God has placed it in the human heart in order to draw man to the One who alone can fulfill it."[8] We might call the mountain we are climbing Mt. Beatitude, or Mt. True Happiness, for that is what it signifies. Reaching the top of Mt. Everest brought Sir Edmund Hillary happiness, but the sublime happiness that comes to those who have learned to follow the Beatitudes dwarfs any happiness to be found on Mt. Everest.

Like any good map for reaching the top of a mountain, the Beatitudes show us the shortest and easiest route to follow. "Blessed are the poor in spirit," "Blessed are the meek," "Blessed are the merciful..." are but signposts along the way to guide our passage. There are, of course, alternative routes that appear along the path to the top—possible shortcuts, detours, more interesting ways of reaching happiness. We are certainly free to choose them. One of our richest endowments is our freedom. Indeed, happiness would not be meaningful if we did not have that freedom. But the other possible ways to the top are illusory. They may offer tentative experiences of what we are seeking, but as we journey on we know what St. Thomas Aquinas meant when he said, "God alone satisfies." The Beatitudes are the way to reach God who alone is complete happiness.

As every mountain trekker knows, there are times when doubts about the accuracy of the map creep in. Is the map perhaps out of date? Has the trail been changed? Am I really getting any closer to my destination? Certainly, we have encountered these doubts in our own spiritual lives, not just on a mountain hike. There is one way to get through such crises of confidence, when it seems the map of Mt. Beatitude is inadequate. It helps to remember that the Beatitudes are also a character sketch, an autobiography of Jesus himself. If we believe that Jesus was perfect Beatitude, then we need only to become familiar with his life in order to renew our confidence in the words he gave us. A deep familiarity with the Gospel is the best assurance that the map is reliable.

The ascent of any great mountain is usually not accomplished alone. Sir Edmund Hillary had the support of many people, in particular a loyal band of Sherpas led by Tensing Norgay. Without their help, Edmund Hillary would not have become Sir Edmund Hillary. And so it is for us on our ascent of Mt. Beatitude. We too receive substantial help on the journey, both from visible and invisible sources. We journey upward on the prayers of the Church, the sacraments, the intercession of the saints, especially Mary. But there is another source of support on our climb, a source that might be analogous to the Sherpas who aided Sir Edmund Hillary. I mean the angels.

There is in our Catholic tradition a fascinating theology of angels, the study of them (angelology), and the part they play in helping us along the spiritual path.[9] Although Christ is our primary guide, angels can be thought of as theophanies or paths to the divine. They illuminate our way, provide guidance or spiritual assistance, sanctify, and manifest power.[10] All of this they do not so humans may worship *them*, but that we may worship the *Trinity*. As we move up the path of Mt. Beatitude, we are aided by the various orders of angels, each of them especially suited to complement our spiritual gifts. St. Bonaventure says the "angelic hierarchy" becomes interiorized and "the effect is of a developmental process of spiritual growth within the human person that parallels the ascent within the angelic hierarchy to God."[11]

How good it is to know that we do not travel the path to perfect happiness alone! We are supported by a host of heavenly guides who know the way and will accompany us every step of the way.

See you at the top!

Questions for Further Discussion:

1. Is the image of the Beatitudes as a road map to the spiritual heights meaningful to you?

2. Have you thought about the angels as beings guides and sources of support on your journey along the spiritual path?

17
THE SALT OF NONVIOLENCE
Fifth Sunday in Ordinary Time (A)

- Isaiah 58:7–10
- 1 Corinthians 2:1–5
- Matthew 5:13–16

Salt.

In the highly seasoned world of the twenty-first century, it is hard to appreciate the universal value salt had when today's Gospel was written. To the ancient world, salt was like gold. Without a kitchen drawer of spices, with no refrigeration or freeze-drying, salt made life more livable.

Salt brought a little flavor to an otherwise bland diet. Salt preserved foods. Roman soldiers sometimes received their pay in rations of salt. No wonder, then, that Jesus would reach for it in describing his followers—"You are the salt of the earth" (Matt 5:13). What a compliment!

Like so much of what Jesus said, however, this line contains a barb, a hook that snags the conscience. If we are attentive, it sticks there and will not be easily dislodged until it has had its intended effect.

Jesus was no easygoing flatterer. No politician. He did not use feel-good language. He follows his complimentary words with this reminder: Salt can lose its taste, it can become good for nothing.

Indeed, it may degrade to the point where it must be tossed out and trampled underfoot.

We would love to hear our Lord refer to us as "the salt of the earth." And he does intend these words for us, sitting here in a church not far from the Great Salt Lake. But are we willing to ponder all the words we just heard? Or will we simply relegate them to that dusty shelf in our minds where so many other platitudes are stored?

I suppose biblical scholars, preachers, teachers have written and spoken a million words about what it means to be "the salt of the earth." Identifying salt with virtue, with living the Christian life, making a difference in our community, with being the seasoning to our world—all of these come easily to mind. They are valid and on another day I might turn to them. But this morning I want to hold up a different salt image, something I consider vital for our times. I want to speak to you about the salt of nonviolence.

I speak of the salt of nonviolence, for I am convinced it is a key ingredient for any follower of Christ. Moreover, I believe it is a Christian ingredient that, over the centuries, has been leeched out of our preaching and our practice. In a world filled with wars—wars against terrorism, preemptive wars, wars to spread democracy and to preserve the American way of life—the salt of nonviolence is a rare commodity. And yet it is the one thing that we Catholic Christians should be offering the world. The world does not need our technology, our smart bombs, our marvelous munitions. The world does not need our consumer culture, our latest rock stars, our pornography. What our world needs is a generous portion of nonviolence. We live in a world that is salt-deprived, a world that desperately needs the salt of nonviolence. If our world is to be preserved from final destruction it will be through nonviolence.

Where will it come from?

There once was a man who knew the value of salt. He was willing to risk his life for it. He lived in a very poor country where salt was scarce and could only be obtained at a high price from an oppressive regime. One day, this man said, "We will get our own salt. We will march to the sea and make salt." This man, of course, was Mahatma Gandhi, one of the few men who fit our Lord's description—Gandhi was the salt of the earth. Gandhi's March to the Sea was one part of his campaign of nonviolence that eventually freed his people from British domination and occupation—an occupation still in effect in Northern Ireland, for example.

Gandhi learned about nonviolence from Jesus Christ. Though a Hindu, and a lawyer, Gandhi first encountered the truth of nonviolence in the *Christian* scriptures. There he discovered and took to heart something we still struggle to realize in our lives—*Jesus was nonviolent.* Jesus taught his followers to love, which is another way of saying he taught them to be nonviolent. Gandhi said once, "Jesus lived and died in vain if He did not teach us to regulate the whole of life by the eternal law of love."[12]

The central message of the gospel is nonviolence, because the gospel is about love, self-sacrificing love. The love Jesus preached and practiced was a love that valued the life of another, even one's enemies, more highly than one's own life. Jesus revealed the truth about God and about human nature. And that truth is this: At the heart of God and nature is love, not hatred; nonviolence, not violence. The more committed we are to living lives of nonviolence, the more we realize this truth.

Our early Church was a nonviolent church. The Church of the catacombs, the Church of Saints Agnes, Perpetua, Agatha, Felicity was a Church in which the salt of nonviolence was integral to life. But with few exceptions, our church since then has chosen a salt-free diet. In our own times, it took a man from a non-Christian tradition to articulate truths that were entrusted to us by Christ. Gandhi wrote:

> [Jesus] a man who was completely innocent, offered himself as a sacrifice for the good of others, including his enemies, and became the ransom of the world. It was a perfect act.[13]

> Jesus was the most active resister known perhaps to history. This was non-violence par excellence.[14]

> Non-violence succeeds only when we have a living faith in God.[15]

There is great hope in hearing the message of Christ articulated by someone from a different religious tradition. And yet it is a bit humbling. Why have *we* not done the same?

One reason may be that we mistake nonviolence for passive resistance, or even cowardice. It is neither. The way of nonviolence can only be followed by those who are brave.

Only those have the courage of their conviction that love is at the heart of all things can put into practice what Jesus taught.

Only those who believe in God and trust in the truth revealed by Christ can willingly make the ultimate sacrifice of themselves to change a world pervaded by violence.

Only those who have meditated on the nonviolent teaching of the gospel and have put it into practice in their daily lives can be called the salt of the earth.

Questions for Further Discussion:

1. Do you think it is possible to live a nonviolent life? How?

2. Can you think of others besides Gandhi who lived lives of non-violence?

PART FOUR

Lent

HOMILIES 18–24

Too late have I loved you, O Beauty so ancient and so new, too late have I loved you! Behold, you were within me, while I was outside: it was there that I sought you, and, a deformed creature, rushed head-long upon these things of beauty which you have made. You were with me, but I was not with you. They kept me far from you, those fair things which, if they were not in you, would not exist at all. You have called to me, and I have cried out, and have shattered my deaf-ness. You have blazed forth with light, and have shone upon me, and you have put my blindness to flight! You have sent forth fragrance, and I have drawn in my breath, and I pant after you. I have tasted you, and I hunger and thirst after you. You have touched me, and I have burned for your peace.

The Confessions of St. Augustine[1]

18

LEAVE YOUR BURDENS AT THE RIVERBANK
Ash Wednesday (A)

> • Joel 2:12–18
> • 2 Corinthians 5:20—6:2
> • Matthew 6:1–6, 16–18

One of my favorite stories from the desert fathers concerns a wise old monk and a younger monk who, like each of us, still had things to learn about spiritual health. Recovering spiritual health, after all, is what Lent is all about.

The story goes like this. The two monks were walking along a road, when they came to a wide riverbank. To their astonishment, a beautiful young woman was sitting on the river bank, unable to cross on her own. She was an attractive woman and scantily clad: someone every good monk should presumably avoid, if he wished to maintain his spiritual health. As the two monks approached, the woman began to weep and to plead with the monks to help her across the stream.

To the younger monk's amazement, the older monk, without hesitating, scooped the woman up in his arms and carried her across, placing her gently on the opposite bank. Then, the two monks continued their journey.

As the two continued on, the younger monk began to fret to himself about what the older monk had just done. Finally, after several miles, when he could stand it no longer, the younger monk blurted out, "How could you touch that woman, and even carry her in your arms?" The older monk considered his visibly upset brother monk for a moment and then said, "I left that woman back there on the riverbank. You have carried her all this way. It must make you very tired."

My friends, Ash Wednesday, the start of Lent, is a time to leave your burdens on this side of the river. In forty days, we will have crossed the great river of Lent. Don't carry needless burdens with you into Easter. Leave them here on this side of Easter.

What needless burdens, you ask? And what do you mean, "Leave them here on the riverbank of Lent?"

Each of us comes to this Lent carrying his or her peculiar burden. A changed attitude toward that burden is what I mean when I say, "Leave it behind."

What needless burdens? Let me name a few I have carried through many past Lents; see if you recognize them. Judging others. Feeling sorry for myself. Bitterness. Grudges nursed over many years. Resentment. Envy. Anger, sometimes expressed, usually concealed in polite irritation. Anxiety. Worry. Preoccupation with desires for material things. Lust.

Need I go on? There are burdens aplenty and each of us has a fair number particularly suited to our individual personality, station in life, and life experience. Like the younger monk, we have picked up these burdens in our minds and find it difficult to leave them on the riverbank.

How to leave them behind?

Now, don't be discouraged with what I am going to say. But, in truth, for as long as we live in this world, we cannot completely leave behind these burdens. But we can lighten the load. We can lighten the load so considerably that, in comparison to the past, it will seem as though we were carrying feathers. It is our attitude toward our burdens that affects their gravity. We might say, then, that Lent is about attitude adjustment.

In her great wisdom, the Church prescribes three means of lightening our burden. Like all wisdom, these prescriptions are paradoxical. I mean that, instead of *lightening* our burdens, these actions would seem to *add* to our burdens. They are, of course, prayer, fasting, and almsgiving. And, because we are human, they *do* seem like additional burdens, which is why we avoid them until our Church tells us to take them up.

And yet, properly understood, each of these practices can change our attitude toward the suffering that results from carrying the dull weight of envy, anger, and all the other burdens. Take fasting, for example. How can fasting help us to leave our burdens on the Lenten riverbank? Much could be said at many levels about the effect of fasting on our spiritual health, but let me mention just one. Fasting is a deliberate choice we make. Making deliberate choices is the key to letting go of our burdens.

There are, of course, burdens that we do not choose: sickness, accidents, genetic defects. But *most* of the burdens we carry are on our shoulders because we choose to place them there. For reasons too complicated to go into here, we choose our own misery, much of the time.[2] We *choose* to let anger fester. We *choose* to place ourselves in situations that will lead to the burden of addiction. We *choose* to find fault with others, to compare ourselves with others, and to make judgments. *Most of the burdens we carry are self-chosen.*

And here is how fasting helps us. By *choosing* to fast, we are taught at a deeper and deeper level that we can choose what our attitude will be. Fasting is a small burden we choose to accept. We choose to forgo eating or drinking, and, in doing so, we begin to realize that we do have power over how we feel. We choose to fast, and we can choose not to fast. Slowly, this discipline awakens us to this awareness: We can choose to stop being angry, stop being jealous or petty. We can choose (at least to some extent) to stop being anxious. We can choose to leave behind the burdens we otherwise might carry into Easter.

This is what Jesus was talking about in today's Gospel. We can choose to make a display of our burdens, whether it be the burdens of anxiety and worry or the burden of fasting. Or we can choose another attitude. We can take up an attitude toward our burden that is so transforming, no one will notice we are carrying it. The remedy the Church prescribes in fasting is a deliberate choice to change our attitude toward the burdens of life.

Prayer. Again, we can make a deliberate choice, an elegant choice, to turn off the TV and spend time with a good spiritual book, which usually leads into prayer—lifting our heart and mind to God. Fasting is the practical way of preparing ourselves for prayer. Fasting frees us from the distraction of nagging burdens and allows us to enter peacefully and joyfully into prayerful communion with God.

Almsgiving, I believe, flows from the first two practices. As we lighten the burden we have placed on ourselves and enter more deliberately into prayer, we begin to lose our taste for the many products, gadgets, and toys our consumer society offers. We begin to live more simply, less encumbered by things. From that comes an awareness of how much we have and how much we can do to affect the lives of individuals carrying real burdens, not only across the river of Lent and into Easter, but throughout their lives.

We go through life carrying needless burdens. This is the season to make the choices that enable us to be the fully alive humans we were intended by God to be. Lent is a time to shed that extra weight, to put down and not pick up again whatever is burdening us. *This* is the time to leave your burdens on the riverbank.

Questions for Further Discussion:

1. Do you think it is possible to leave your burdens on this side of the river of Lent?

2. Do you see how fasting, prayer, and almsgiving help you during Lent?

19
LENT: A TIME TO BECOME FULLY HUMAN[3]
First Sunday of Lent (A)

- Genesis 2:7–9; 3:1–7
- Romans 5:12–19
- Matthew 4:1–11

There was a time when our race walked in harmony with God. A time when our race was content with being simply human.

There was a time when representatives of our race walked arm in arm with God in the stillness and beauty of a garden, a paradise stirred only by the gentle breezes that moved like the Spirit upon the waters. It was a time of peace, with Creator and created united in perfect love.

There was a time when our race was fully human, depending on God the way the earth depends on the heavens for rain, the way plants depend on the earth and the sun for nourishment, the way earthen vessels wait patiently until they are filled.

There came a time when our race first faced temptation. A tempter was allowed into paradise, raising insidious doubts in the minds of our ancestors. The temptation: Be like gods.

The tempter whispered: Do not be content with being simply human, with being dependent on God. Be like gods yourselves!

And our race, gifted by God with freedom, gave in to that temptation and lost its perfect relationship with God. It was the time of the Great Separation. Our race rebelled against being simply human, choosing, instead, to be like gods.

But God did not remain aloof from a world corrupted by the chaos of human freedom. There came a time, not that long ago in the history of salvation, when another man, a Jewish man, a simple man from Galilee, faced again the temptation that first beguiled our race. Jesus of Nazareth, his locks still damp from baptism in the Jordan, his ears still ringing with the words from heaven—"This is my Son, the Beloved"—left the crowds and made his way into the loneliness of the desert to face the temptation we all must face: *Will you take up the chalice of being human or will you try to be like gods?*

But something is different this time. This time the tempter knows he is not dealing with the innocent representatives of our race but with a wise and holy man who knows the scriptures as well as he knows the human condition. So the tempter comes at him from three different angles. He knows that when a man or woman fasts, the poverty of the human condition can be too much. And so he says to Jesus, You don't have to accept the poverty of being human, you have the power to turn these stones into bread. Just do it, no one will notice.

But this is no ordinary man. Jesus chooses to remain faithful to his humanity and replies, As a true human, I do not live on bread alone but on the word of God.

Foiled by this perfect response, the tempter tries another angle. Make a display of your divine power, Jesus, show the Romans what a simple Galilean can do. Think of it, Jesus, you can do something your ancestors could not do: drive out these hated Romans, restore Israel to its divinely ordained power and glory. And Jesus says to the tempter, I *am* human. I will accomplish my mission as a human. I will carry out my obscure mission as a human. I will carry it out all the way to Calvary, where I will reveal what real power is. On the cross, I will show you what it means to be fully human.

Finally, the tempter tries the temptation that has to be the most seductive, because it is so pervasive in our world—serve someone *other* than God, worship lesser gods and I will give you all the kingdoms of the world in their magnificence. And Jesus responds with what is the key to restoring our race to its full humanity: "The Lord, your God, shall you worship and him alone shall you serve" (Matt 4:10). In essence, the Hebrew Shema: "Hear, O Israel: The Lord is our God, the Lord alone. You shall love the Lord your God with all your heart, and with all your soul, and with all your might" (Deut 6:4 NRSV).

There is a time in the liturgical year of the Church when we, like Jesus, go into the desert for forty days to face temptation. That time is called Lent. We go into our Lenten desert to struggle more purposefully, more mindfully, with the same fundamental temptation our early ancestors faced: the temptation to be like gods.

The temptations we face are usually not gross ones. It is unlikely we will be tempted to turn stones into bread. The temptations that come to us are more subtle and refined; they are perfectly crafted to fit our individual weaknesses, our peculiar fears, our unique needs. We live in a world of designer temptations.

We may be quite capable of dealing with physical hunger, but what about the other hungers: the hunger of lust, the hunger for power, for control, for absolute security, the hunger to be somebody. These are the hungers, these are the temptations that keep us from being fully human. Lent is simply the means the Church gives us to be more attentive to the temptations that deprive us of our full humanity. If we are faithful to the Lenten practices of fasting, prayer, and alms-giving, we become more capable of identifying and arresting our unique temptations.

A marvelous thing happens when through the discipline of Lent we become more aware of what it means to be fully human. We begin to rediscover the closeness with God our race once enjoyed. We come to experience the peace that is rightfully ours when we live in rela-tionship with God. We come to know the joy of being simply human rather than trying to be like gods.

We do not walk through this Lenten desert alone. If we are atten-tive, we will see the tracks of Jesus at every turn. Jesus walked into the desert of our human condition and altered forever the geography of our being. He has gone before us, showing us the way, giving us courage, making it possible for us to overcome temptation, showing us how to be fully human. Paul says that through the obedience of Jesus our race was set right with God. Paul's headline reads: "Human Race Acquitted!" And that's good news.

We do not take on these Lenten obligations solely for our indi-vidual good. We do it for the whole human race.

There will come a time when Lent will end. Liturgically, it ends on Holy Thursday. More importantly, it will end at some time for each of us individually and for our race. There will come a time when we will again be fully human, fully capable of living in perfect, loving union with God. May our Lenten practices hasten the coming of that day.

Questions for Further Discussion:

1. Have you thought of Christ's temptations in the desert as being temptations to not accept his humanity? Do you ever face these temptations?

2. What does it mean to become fully human?

20
TRANSCENDENCE
Second Sunday of Lent (A)

- Genesis 12:1–4a
- 2 Timothy 1:8b–10
- Matthew 17:1–9

Today's Gospel is about transcendence. The Winter Olympics, too, are about transcendence.

In the Gospel, Matthew describes the transfiguration of Jesus as witnessed by Peter, James, and John. For the three disciples, it was an experience of Olympian proportions. For a brief time, Jesus transcended the temporal limits of human existence; everything about him revealed the glory of God. And it must have deepened the three disciples' own longing for transcendence.

The longing for transcendence, that insatiable desire to go beyond ourselves, is part of our nature. We are made in the image of God and our deepest desire is for God. Each of our lives is a unique account of our longing and striving to transcend whatever keeps us from God. The determined desire of Olympic athletes to overcome human limitations is but a sign that points to our own desire for transcendence. We have an infinite capacity for transcendence.

Events of human accomplishment, such as the Winter Olympics, are always about transcendence. How, then, do they teach us about transcendence? In the hospitality that is demanded of the host city, we experience a kind of transcendence.

The Olympics have meaning on an even higher level, for in showing us the limits of human accomplishment, they remind us that our longing for transcendence can only be satisfied in God. For many years, we have thrilled at the artistic performance of Michelle Kwan, the publicly acclaimed Queen of Women's Figure Skating. But now, Michelle, only twenty-five years old, has been edged out by twenty-one-year-old Sara Hughes. In a few years, Sara Hughes too will be displaced. There is in every great human accomplishment a mixture of joy and melancholy, a kind of tension between glory and sadness, for we know that our greatest human accomplishments cannot satisfy our longing for transcendence. We sense, albeit vaguely at times, that our capacity for transcendence is intended for God alone.

Fortunately, it is not an either/or situation. It is not a case of rejecting great human accomplishment in favor of an exclusive reaching for God. It is a both/and situation. When we experience the excitement of a Picabo Street striving to surpass human limitation in downhill skiing, when we thrill at the elegant movement of Sara, or Michelle, or Sasha, we know what the poet Gerard Manley Hopkins meant when he said all the world is charged with the grandeur of God. There is nothing profane in the world, for those who have eyes to see. Perhaps even curling can lift our minds to God. But I doubt it.

To what then do these signs of human transcendence point us? They point us, first of all, to the presence of God within all of our human activities. Whenever we "go for the gold" in our particular vocation in this life, we are striving to transcend our human limitations. When we do that, we experience ecstasy. Like the transfigured Christ, we step out of the ordinary and the mundane and into the glory of God. Any time we go beyond ourselves in loving others, we experience transcendence, be it ever so brief.

The signs of transcendence point us as well to the sacred events of life where we experience the transcendent Christ. Christ came into the world to make it possible for us to transcend all human limitations. In the sacraments, especially in the Eucharist, we enter more deeply into Christ. In doing so, we experience transcendence of the highest kind.

The Olympics remind us of something else of critical importance: the reality of sin and human frailty. One of the most beautiful Olympic events—the paired skating—was marred by controversy in the 2002 Winter Olympics. Allegations of human frailty in judging opened up a controversy that cast a shadow over a beautiful performance. This too reminds us that our best efforts will always be limited by the presence of sin in the world. In seeking to transcend human limitations, Olympic athletes struggle against the force of gravity; in our journey to God, we struggle against the forces of sin and evil, which are always tugging at us and holding us back from the transcendence we long for.

But we have something going for us that will make the difference: Christian hope. On this planet, athletes can never overcome the pull of gravity. But we *can* overcome the power of sin. Christ has conquered sin and death, making it possible for us to leap beyond the limits of sin and soar to transcendent heights. The saints are witnesses to that. It is possible, because Christ has redeemed our world. The stopwatch that signals the limits of human capacity does not apply to our striving for God. The Olympic symbols of rings and blazing torches are good at one level; but for Christians, the central symbol will always be the cross of Christ.

The closing ceremony of the Winter Olympics is the final event. It is tempting to think of this as a sign pointing to the ultimate experience of transcendence that comes with death. But I would offer an alternative interpretation of this symbol. For us, the final ceremony can be whenever we realize that no human accomplishment can satisfy our longing for transcendence. When we realize that truth, we are able to place in proper perspective the things we strive for. This realization can happen at any time. It can happen especially in the Eucharist.

May this Eucharist today be a partial satisfaction of our longing for transcendence; may it strengthen us to excel in all the events of our ordinary lives; may it bring us at last to union with God, the end of our longing for transcendence.

Questions for Further Discussion:

1. Do you experience yourself as striving for transcendence? In what ways?

2. Why are we unable to experience true transcendence in this life?

21
THE UNNAMED HEROINE OF SAMARIA
Third Sunday of Lent (A)

- Exodus 17:3–7
- Romans 5:1–2, 5–8
- John 4:5–42

If I should ever become pope—and I'm positive the chances of that happening are at best pretty remote—I would declare a feast day to celebrate the unnamed woman in today's Gospel. What a remarkable model she is for us: a woman of courage, a woman who teaches us about human dignity and about the conversion process we undergo throughout our lives.

First, a word about her courage. Think for a moment about the obstacles this woman had to overcome. In the culture of her time, it was unheard of for a woman to speak to a man in public—even her husband. It probably says something about the human character of Jesus that she had the courage to speak to him at all. There must have been something about him that allowed her to overcome that barrier.

Then there is the obstacle of her being a Samaritan and Jesus a Jew. I suppose the divide between these two religious groups was like that which has existed between Catholics and Protestants in Northern Ireland. After the breakup of the Kingdom of Israel, the people of Samaria were despised by the Jews of Israel. Although they shared a common background in history and faith, the Samaritans were looked down on as Jews who had assimilated to and been corrupted by conquering forces. Again, it is to the Samaritan woman's credit that she overcame this obstacle.

And then what must have been the greatest obstacle of all: living with the label of having had five husbands. It is hard to believe that John has it right. Remember that, at the time of Jesus, it was the man who had the authority to divorce his wife. This unnamed Samaritan woman had been rejected five times. I doubt that I would have the courage to speak to anyone if I had to live with the stigma attached to this woman. And perhaps that is why she is at the well at midday, rather than in the cool of the morning or evening when most other women would have come there.

We need the Samaritan woman to teach us about courage, courage to overcome obstacles and respond to Christ. No matter how long we have been Catholic, no matter how religious and holy we are, Jesus still remains something of a stranger to us. We spend our lives coming to know Christ. It takes courage to overcome the obstacles in our lives that keep us from responding to Christ in the way this Samaritan woman did. Those obstacles are many and varied. We may be someone who lives with a label, just like the Samaritan woman. Perhaps we feel *unworthy* to approach Christ. The Samaritan woman teaches us that *we need not be afraid,* we need not hold back. Christ used the human need for water to reach out to the Samaritan woman. Perhaps we need to ask: What need is Jesus using in my life to establish that same kind of relationship with me?

We need the Samaritan woman to teach us one of the fundamental principles of Catholic teaching on social justice. Simply stated, the principle is this: Every person, regardless of creed, color, or circumstance, shares in the dignity of God. The Samaritan woman, like each of us, was created in the image and likeness of God. When Christ saw her, he saw her dignity, not the incidental aspects of her life. Jesus saw someone who shared in his own dignity, both human and divine.

We need the Samaritan woman to teach us about the lifelong process of conversion. Our lives follow the same pattern as that displayed so beautifully in the story of the Samaritan woman. We hear the call of Christ. We have the courage to respond. We begin to realize our own innate human dignity. We respond in prayer, both with words and without. And then suddenly something happens: The encounter with Jesus suddenly moves to a new level.

We see this happening to the Samaritan woman. She begins by talking about water, about cisterns and wells. But gradually, Jesus begins to speak to an area of her life that she thought was hidden. He addresses the shadow side of her life: the five husbands. There is a subtle hint of humor in how he does this. He shows that he appreciates and understands her and, yet, does not reject her.

Now, the woman's understanding takes off: You are a prophet, you are the Messiah, you are the Christ. The Samaritan woman's world would never be the same again, nor would her community. When Christ speaks to the deepest, most hidden part of our lives, we are never the same again. And neither is our community. When we have the courage to enter into a relationship with Christ, something begins to happen. We become transformed people, people who can be evangelists to a community.

Every journey to Christ follows in some way the path this woman took. It involves a descent into ourselves where we overcome, with the help of Christ, whatever obstacle that is holding us back. And then it becomes an ascent into a new and transformed life. A genuine encounter with Christ always results in our returning to the community a changed person, ready to be a transforming agent ourselves. And that, in essence, is the Catholic approach to social justice. Transformed by an ever-deepening encounter with Christ, we see more clearly the dignity of each person. More fully conscious of our dignity discovered in Christ, we are drawn to change those conditions that diminish the human dignity of others.

Salvation history is full of unnamed, unsung heroines. The Samaritan woman is one of the greatest. She teaches us about courage, about human dignity, about conversion and what it means to be in relationship with Christ. We join now with her, with all holy men and women, with the saints and angels, in thanking God through the Eucharist.

Questions for Further Discussion:

1. Have you thought before of the Samaritan woman as a heroine, a woman of courage, a model for spiritual growth? How is she usually presented?

2. What does it mean that our path to Christ is a descent into ourselves and then an ascent into a new and transformed life? Have you experienced this in some way?

22

I GET NO RESPECT
Fourth Sunday of Lent (A)

> • 1 Samuel 6:1b, 6–7, 10–13a
> • Ephesians 5:8–14
> • John 9:1–41

The comedian Rodney Dangerfield was famous for his line, "I get no respect." One of the self-effacing stories he told is how as a child he got lost at the state fair. Feeling desperate, he went to a policeman and asked for help in finding his parents. After searching for a while, Rodney asks the policeman, "Do you think we will find my parents?" The officer replies, "I don't know, kid, there are so many places where they could hide."

I get no respect!

Today's readings teach us about respect. Not respect in the way we usually think of the word, not in the sense of the respect we give to someone in a position of authority. I am using the word *respect* in an alternative, more basic way. *Respect* comes from the Latin word, *respicere*, which means to look back at, to look at a second time. In other words, to look more closely, more deeply. That is the kind of respect God reveals in the readings; and it is the kind of respect we secretly long for as a holy people of God.

We see in the first reading from Samuel a wonderful example of God's respect. In this story, Jesse presents to Samuel each of his seven older sons only to discover that it was his youngest son, David, who is to be anointed king of Israel. The prophet Samuel says it so clearly: "Not as man sees does God see, because man sees the appearance but the Lord looks into the heart" (1 Sam 16:7).

Bible stories do not always grab our attention; they may seem distant and irrelevant to our lives. So let me retell the story in a modern context. Imagine that the United States has become a theocracy—a country ruled by God. Now imagine that the chief justice of the Supreme Court is also a prophet, like Samuel. Under this theocracy, the chief justice is required by the Constitution to go out and search for the future president of the country. You are the father, or mother, of a large, Catholic family and one day the chief justice appears at your door. He announces who he is and that his mission is to locate the next president.

You are overwhelmed by the thought that one of your sons might be president and you proudly present them, one by one. The first is an excellent student, straight A's and a scholarship to Notre Dame. The second is not only a scholar but also a fine athlete. And so on down the line. But none of the seven sons satisfies the chief justice. Finally, he asks you, "Are these *all* your children?" You hesitate and then admit, "Well, there is my youngest child—equally bright and capable—but, you see, my youngest is a girl. I have a daughter." And, of course, you know how the story ends. The chief justice declares that this girl is to be a future president of the country.

Now you look on your daughter in a different way; you begin to have real respect for her. You look again, you look more deeply, more closely than ever before. Now you begin to see as God sees, not just outward appearances; you look past outer appearances to the heart. You have real respect.

What a freeing moment it is when we realize that God looks at the heart. When we come to this realization, we can look at our children in a new way. We can stop judging them by what they have done, or haven't done. We can relax in the knowledge that this son or daughter, who might seem unaccomplished by the standards of the world, is seen by God in an entirely different way. God does not glance at this child's outer appearance, as we so often do; God gives a long, loving gaze at the heart of this child. And God sees there the image of God. God does this with each and every one of us. God has true respect for us; God cannot stop gazing lovingly upon creation.

Sometimes God even uses the comic strips to teach us how to see. The comic strip, "Family Circle," which often has some good theology in it, once showed the little boy, Jeff, looking out a window and exclaiming excitedly, "Look at all the birds, all the flowers and things out there." Then, his sister comes to the window and says, "Look at all the dust, the smudges and the finger prints on this window." As Jeff walks away, he says, "Don't you know, windows are for looking through, not at."

We all want to have that kind of vision. We want to get beyond our prejudices, our biases, our fears and see people, all of creation, as God does. This is a part of our constant longing to be a holy people. But how do we do it?

The answer lies in the long story of the man healed of his blindness in today's Gospel. The story teaches us that it is only by coming to faith in Jesus Christ that our vision can be fully restored.

This is a story intended specifically for the members of our community who will be entering the Church at Easter, our elect and candidates. Depictions of this story appear seven times in the catacombs at Rome. The depictions are always associated with baptism: The man is sent to wash in the waters of Siloam, reminding us of our own baptism. And the story is about enlightenment, about seeing more clearly, about respect.

To the Pharisees, the man in today's Gospel was a true Rodney Dangerfield. He gets no respect. To most of the Pharisees he is seen as a sinner, an impostor, a fool. Who respects this man? *Jesus* does. Jesus looks on him with the loving gaze of God and not only heals him of his physical blindness, but brings him to faith in Christ. Notice that when first asked who healed him, the man replies: "The man called Jesus" did it; later, he says of Jesus, "He is a prophet." Still later, he acknowledges Jesus as Son of Man. And finally he says simply, "I do believe, Lord" (John 9:38). The text continues, "And he worshiped him." This is a synopsis of our growth in faith, growth that takes a lifetime.

So how do we come to see as God sees? By drawing closer to Christ in faith. It starts with baptism but it is a lifelong process of giving our hearts to Christ. An intellectual knowledge of the historical Jesus is not enough. An acknowledgment of Jesus as a prophet, as the greatest man who ever lived is not enough. It is only when we are able to say, "Jesus is Lord," and mean it, that we make the breakthrough into seeing as God does. Then we experience true respect.

Questions for Further Discussion:

1. Have you thought of respect as looking again at someone, looking more deeply? Whom do you respect? Do you get respect?

2. Do you see the progression in the blind man's understanding of Jesus? Can you apply it to your own life?

23
FAITH IN THE FAMILY
Fifth Sunday of Lent (A)

* Ezekiel 37:12–14
* Romans 8:8–11
* John 11:1–45

Given the success Mel Gibson has had with his movie, *The Passion of the Christ*, I have decided to write a screenplay of my own. I heard recently that Mel Gibson had grossed something like $350 million on his movie. If I could get just 1 percent of that, Mary Lou and I could retire to a château in the south of France!

The screenplay is based on today's Gospel and has the tentative working title, *Faith in the Family*. It will dramatize the relationship that Lazarus, Martha, and Mary had with Jesus and will explore how their relationships can teach us about our own coming to faith. The story is set in Bethany, two miles from Jerusalem. It consists of five scenes, depicting events from today's Gospel and Luke's Gospel, chapter 10, verses 38–42.

Scene One: A small room in the home of Lazarus, Mary, and Martha

Jesus is seated at a table with Lazarus. They are enjoying a bit of wine and bread. They laugh heartily as they share jokes, puns, stories, and the simple joy of being in each other's company. Through dialogue, the audience will come to understand why Jesus wept at the death of Lazarus and why it was said, "See how he loved him."

Scene Two: The living room in the home of Lazarus, Mary, and Martha

In this scene, Jesus is seated talking quietly to Mary, who is at his feet, listening intently to what he has to say. Martha is hurrying about, showing frustration at Mary's apparent lack of compassion for her, as she works to make everything perfect for the Teacher. Jesus teases Martha about her need to be the perfect hostess.

What the audience will learn from Martha's dialogue with Jesus in this scene is that her compassion will become truly fruitful when she learns to waste time with the Lord, the way Mary has been doing. But, then, Jesus will also remind Mary that her contemplation at his feet must lead her into real compassion for those around her. Anticipating

Thomas Merton, Jesus reminds Mary, "There is no theology of prayer that is not a theology of compassion."[4]

Scene Three: The tomb where Lazarus has been buried

It is now several weeks later, and Jesus has arrived at the tomb. The dialogue is based on the words of today's Gospel. The main interaction is between Jesus and Martha. The dialogue begins with Martha's words to Jesus, "Lord, if you had been here, my brother would not have died" (John 11:20). Through the dialogue that follows, Jesus helps Martha to understand that, because of his presence in the world, eternal life is *now*! In this scene, Martha, representing all of us, will come to see more clearly that eternal life is not just something to be experienced at the end of time, as Martha mistakenly assumes when she says, "I know that he will rise, in the resurrection on the last day" (John 11:24). Jesus will say to Martha, and to us, "Eternal life is now; you only have to realize it!" The audience will learn from this scene that, by being fully present to the risen Lord, we begin already in this life to experience the power of the resurrection. For Martha, it took the shocking death of her brother, Lazarus, to draw her out of her busy lifestyle so that she might realize the empowering presence of Christ, the source of eternal life.

Scene Four: The home of Lazarus, Mary, and Martha

In this scene, Lazarus, Mary, and Martha are shown walking slowly away from Bethany. Jesus is seated alone at the table. He is bent forward, his face sad and tired. In the distance, shrouded in mist, can be seen a cross. In the back of the scene, a chorus of bearded men in dark robes can be heard plotting the death of Jesus. They can be heard saying that this man cannot be allowed to continue teaching "eternal life is now." To permit such heresy would mean the end of the established system of religion.

Scene Five: The west sacristy of St. Joseph Church

This scene is staged to look exactly like the west sacristy of our very own St. Joseph Church, including the ladder leaning against the wall, the unused flowers, the chairs in a circle. The elect enter quietly and take their seats. Then, Lazarus, Mary, and Martha come into the sacristy and take their seats with the elect. They begin to tell the elect about their relationship with Jesus and how it brought them to faith. Lazarus will talk excitedly about the wonderfully human Jesus and how knowing Jesus in his humanity is the start of coming to believe in him. Martha will tell the elect how being fully present to Jesus led her to experience eternal life now. And Mary will talk about the importance of getting up from the feet of Jesus to serve others; in other words, to enter into the dynamic of moving from contemplation to compassion, and back again.

So, there you have it: my idea for a screenplay! If it comes out as movie, I hope you will buy a ticket. My retirement depends on it!

Questions for Further Discussion:

1. What changes might you make to the screenplay?
2. Do you find the experiences of Mary, Martha, and Lazarus relevant to your own journey in faith? In what ways?

24
BE FULLY ALIVE, FULLY PASSIONATE
Palm Sunday of the Lord's Passion (A)

- Isaiah 50:4–7
- Philippians 2:6–11
- Matthew 26:14—27:66

In the second century, St. Irenaeus said, "The glory of God is a human being who is fully alive." On this Passion Sunday, we might say, "The glory of God is a human being who is fully passionate."

Passion is one of the greatest gifts God has given us. Passion is the fire that burns in the heart of every human being. Passion is the flame of genius that gives us great music, enduring art, classic literature, and sometimes even inspired preaching.

Jesus came to light a fire upon the earth. That fire is our passion for God!

Jesus was fully human; Jesus was filled with passion. Jesus was the glory of God.

Jesus was a passionate man. Everything that Jesus did bore the mark of his passion: every forgiving word he spoke, every gesture of love, his laughter, his tears, his anger at hypocrisy; everything was fired with passion. The intensity of his will, the depth of his feeling, his love for the poor and vulnerable; everything was fired with his passion.

It was the passion of Jesus that saved us. The passion that burned in the heart of Jesus led him to Gethsemane, to the high priest's house, to the court of Pontius Pilate, to Golgotha. Passion led Christ to the cross.

Jesus was a man of passion. But so was Pontius Pilate. So too were the Jewish authorities. You might say that the passion narrative is a clash of passions. The passion of those who brought about the suffering and death of Jesus was a negative force; it was misdirected, unredeemed passion; it was passion not for God and for life, but for death and destruction. And that is where passion goes when it is not directed ultimately toward God.

What makes the difference? Why was the passion of some directed toward death and destruction while the passion of Jesus was directed toward God?

The answer, I suggest, is found in the reading from Philippians: "Christ Jesus, though he was in the form of God, did not regard equality with God something to be grasped. Rather, he emptied himself, taking the form of a slave, coming in human likeness; and found human in appearance, he humbled himself, becoming obedient to the point of death, even death on a cross" (Phil 2:6–8).

Kenosis is the Greek word for it. Jesus' life was a life of self-emptying. Jesus trusted completely in his Abba, his Father. Our Lenten journey is a journey of *kenosis,* of emptying ourselves of everything that misdirects our passion for God. When we let go of anger, jealousy, envy, hatred, then our passion turns naturally to God. It is in our nature to be wildly passionate about God. Sin blocks that passion.

My friends, be fully human this Holy Week. Be passionate people! Share in the passionate love of Christ for his disciples and his Church on Holy Thursday. Walk with Christ along the way of self-emptying this Good Friday. Walk the path of *kenosis,* of dying to self until it leads to the heights of passion. On Easter morning, let the fire of passion for God erupt in your hearts like the fire of the Easter candle. Let your passion swell like the Exsultet. Be passionate people; be fully human!

Questions for Further Discussion:

1. What does it mean to be fully alive? Why is the fully alive person the glory of God?

2. What aspect of Christ's passion appeals to you the most? How can you become a more passionate person?

PART FIVE

Triduum

The third hour. And the ninth.—They are *here*. And *now*. They *are* now!
"Jesus will be in agony even to the end of the world. We must
not sleep during that time." *(Pascal)*
We must not—And for the watcher is the far-off present—
also present in his contact with mankind among whom,
at every moment, Jesus dies in someone who followed the
trail marks of the inner road to the end:
love and patience,
righteousness and humility,
faith and courage,
stillness.

Dag Hammarskjöld, *Markings*[1]

25

JESUS THE DIVINE PLAYWRIGHT
Holy Thursday (A)

- Exodus 12:1–8, 11–14
- 1 Corinthians 11:23–26
- John 13:1–15

In the history of Western civilization there has been no greater playwright than William Shakespeare. Every summer thousands flock like pilgrims to the Shakespeare festival in Cedar City, Utah. A movie based on Shakespeare won an Academy Award just a few years ago. Even among high school students, Shakespeare has never been more popular. Shakespeare remains popular because he understood human nature and he knew how to dramatize what he understood.

But we have someone greater than Shakespeare here. We have someone who not only understood human nature, because he lived it, but someone who was also divine, living in perfect intimacy with God the Father, someone who knew both humanity and divinity—we have Jesus Christ.

Like a great playwright, Jesus has tried during this Lent, through words and images, to help his followers, including ourselves, to understand who he was, the nature of his mission, and how we must live our lives if we are to experience union with God the Father.

Jesus shocked his Jewish disciples in the scene set at the well, when he talked with a Samaritan woman and told her that he is the living water. But did they understand what he meant when he said whoever drinks of this living water will never thirst again? Do we understand?

Then he gave us the marvelous and dramatic scene set in Jerusalem where sight was restored to a man blind from birth. With an artist's craft, the author of John's Gospel showed us how this man grew in his understanding of Jesus. Do we understand the full implication of the man confessing, "Lord, I believe"?

And then Jesus gave us a scene that should have left no doubt as to who he is and what he was about—he brought his friend Lazarus back to life so that his followers might believe that Jesus is the resurrection and the life. When the curtain closed on that scene, could there possibly have been anyone who did not believe that Jesus was the one sent by God?

Now Jesus appears in the final scene of his ministry. In this evening's Gospel, Jesus gives us a symbolic gesture that not only models the behavior required of his followers but points to the meaning of what will happen tomorrow and the next day, the final acts in this drama of salvation. Jesus did not give his followers an after-dinner speech; he did not put them to sleep with a theological discourse on the meaning of being a Christian. Rather, he did something very deliberate and dramatic. The Gospel writer says,

> He rose from supper...
> Took off his outer garments...
> He took a towel...
> He tied it around his waist...
> He poured water into a basin...
> He began to wash the disciples' feet...
> He dried them with the towel around his waist.

Everything is done to give the most dramatic effect. Why? So that his disciples might remember this scene and, when the final act is finished, that they might understand.

Jesus left his disciples with a dramatic image that must have been shocking, confusing, even embarrassing at the time. It was not customary for the presider to wash the feet of others in the middle of supper. That was the job of a *slave* when guests first arrived at the house. But then, later, looking back they must have understood and been able to sing with St. Paul the great hymn we heard on Passion Sunday:

> Christ Jesus, though he was in the form of God,
>   did not regard equality with God
>   something to be grasped
> Rather, he emptied himself,
>   taking the form of a slave,
>   coming in human likeness;
>   and found human in appearance,
>   he humbled himself,
>   becoming obedient to the point of death,
>   even death on a cross.   (Phil 2:6–8)

When the image of Jesus washing their feet was seen in the light of the resurrection, the disciples would understand.

They would also come to see that this image was not out of place at the Last Supper, a meal we see as the origins of the Eucharist. Christ emptied himself in the incarnation, he emptied himself at Calvary, and he empties himself again and again every time the Eucharist is celebrated. The image of Jesus humbly washing the feet of those he loved is the key to our appreciating the great sacrament we call Eucharist.

But this final scene is not one dominated by Jesus alone. He invites us into the scene as well. He will not let us remain as spectators. He says to us, if you want to taste the living water, if you want to see more clearly, if you want to experience in this life that I am the resurrection, then you must do as I have done. You must take off your outer garments, you must wrap the towel around your waist, and you must wash my feet wherever you find me in your world.

And we are never without opportunities to wash the feet of Jesus, to care for him as he appears in our world disguised as the poor and needy. Shakespeare, with all of his insight, never captured the reality of Jesus among us, begging for us to serve him. Jesus begs us to enter the scenes in our daily lives and wash his feet, for that is the surest way of finding meaning in our lives, in the Eucharist, and in the events that are soon to follow.

Shakespeare places on the lips of Macbeth these words about the meaning of life. He says:

> Life's but a walking shadow, a poor player,
> That struts and frets his hour upon the stage,
> And then is heard no more; it is a tale
> Told by an idiot, full of sound and fury,
> Signifying nothing. (Act V, scene v)

As Catholic Christians, we take a different view of life. We find meaning in life by entering into the life of service to others that Jesus imaged for us. We find meaning in washing the feet of those people in our lives most in need of care. We find meaning in the Eucharist where Christ empties himself and becomes the humble elements of bread and wine. We reply to Shakespeare that life is a great hymn, sung by all of God's saints, living and dead, filled with suffering, but filled also with joy, obscured at times by darkness and apparent defeat but issuing finally into victory over death and eternal life.

Questions for Further Discussion:

1. Which scene from the gospels proclaimed during Lent appealed to you the most? Why?

2. If you were asked to review the work of Jesus, the Divine Playwright, what would you say?

26
KEEPING THE CROSS IN FOCUS
Good Friday (A)

- Isaiah 52:13—53:12
- Hebrews 4:14–16; 5:7–9
- John 18:1—19:42

When I listen to the Gospel narrative we just finished, I find myself thinking of the 3D illusions that artists began producing a few years ago. You may have seen these intricately designed pictures, usually on posters or calendars. If you look at the design one way, you see only lines. But if you turn the picture a certain way, or are able to let your eyes go out of focus, a marvelous three-dimensional picture appears. Today's Gospel is like that. Pilate asks at one point, "What is truth?" And, indeed, it is as though truth were obscured from everyone present.

Pilate is the first example. In a sense, it is hard to place full blame on Pilate for the mockery he made of Jesus, how he had him dressed as a king and made a spectacle of. Pilate was no stranger to the world of power. He had to have been well acquainted with emperors and kings; and the irony of the situation must have been overwhelming for him. A man appears before him with no army, no entourage, no regalia, and is referred to as a *king*!

Pilate could not penetrate the illusion of weakness before him and see that this man he had mocked and scorned was, indeed, a king—a king not only of the Jews, but of all people, all creation.

And Peter. What did he see? Peter must have seen the end of a dream as his dear friend was led off through a mob of hatred and impending violence. With the electricity of danger in the air, who could expect Peter to see clearly. Peter was like one of the survivors of the Titanic, clinging to his little lifeboat, afraid, and thinking only of his own survival.

And then there were the soldiers and the crowds. What did *they* see? They saw the cross. Who could expect them to look at this horrible instrument of cruelty and see in it the symbol of God's love and mercy? For the Jews, death on a cross was a shameful thing. In the world in which the gospels were written, the cross was a source of scandal, a sign of failure, of foolishness. Outside the circles of early Christians, it was against good manners to speak of the cross. It was considered unaesthetic, unrespectable, and perverse.

But by the time today's Gospel was finally written down, maybe forty years later, the scene that unfolded that night had come into better focus. Now, the writer of the Gospel underscores and emphasizes the kingship theme. Unlike Pilate, the author of John's Gospel saw a true king in this horrible scene. A most unusual king, whose strength lay in his apparent weakness and absolute fidelity to his Father, a king who through his self-emptying made salvation possible.

And he saw in the cross the central symbol of Christianity. Not an illusion but a symbol, something that points beyond itself, revealing the true nature of God: a God who suffers and dies in order to give life. A symbol that leads out to the abandoned and the marginalized.

And what do we see when we look at the cross today? As Catholics we cannot let the cross slip out of focus. We cannot let it become something to which we are indifferent, like a piece of jewelry worn for decoration. If we are truly to be called Christians, we must stay focused on the cross.

In the words of Martin Luther, *crux probat omnia*, "the cross tests everything." The cross tests the way we live our daily lives. Do we remain self-centered, or do we go out to others? Do we nurse resentments, or do we offer forgiveness? Do we remain *I*-centered, or do we become more *other*-directed?

The cross tests the way we live in society. Christ was not crucified between two candles in a sanctuary; he was crucified outside the walls between two criminals. If the Church is to be faithful to that dangerous memory, that is where we must find ourselves—among the alienated, the outcasts, those in prison, those who are suffering in our nursing homes, those for whom life is just too much at times. Wherever there is suffering, that is where the symbol of the cross points us.

How do we keep the cross in focus? By *living* it. We cannot come to understand the cross except by participation in Christ's mission. By imitation of Christ's self-emptying, we come to understand the cross.

When we look at the cross from the perspective of Good Friday, it seems dark and foreboding. But we know there is another side to the cross that will come into focus in a few days. The other side of the cross is the cross of hope. We wait now in trust and anticipation for that reality to become clear.

Questions for Further Discussion:

1. Do you think we have become indifferent to the cross? Why or why not?

2. What can you do to keep the cross in focus?

27
WHY ARE YOU WEARING THAT LIFE PRESERVER?
Easter Vigil (A)

- Genesis 1:1—2:2; 22:1–18
- Exodus 14:15—15:1
- Isaiah 54:5–14; 55:1–11
- Baruch 3:9–15, 32—4:4
- Ezekiel 36:16–17a, 18–28
- Romans 6:3–11
- Matthew 28:1–10

We know very little about the resurrection.

We know many of the details of what happened to Jesus during Holy Week. We know about the Last Supper with the disciples, the agony in the garden at Gethsemane, the trial before Pilate, the horrors of Jesus' crucifixion and death. But we know very little about his resurrection. What happened in the tomb between Good Friday and Easter morning? The gospel authors give us no clue. They speak of an empty tomb, of angels, of Jesus appearing to the women. But they say nothing about the actual experience of the resurrection itself.

And perhaps they were silent for a good reason. Perhaps they wanted us to begin shifting our attention from the physical phenomena of Good Friday to the more spiritual experience of resurrection in our own lives. Tonight, we are given a way of approaching that mystery, a way that can open up for us the meaning of resurrection. It is baptism. At this Easter Vigil we will baptize new members into our faith community. The baptism of these elect, as well as our own baptisms that we renew this night, point the way to a deeper understanding of the resurrection.

In his Letter to the Romans, which we just heard, Paul says, "Are you unaware that we who were baptized into Christ Jesus were baptized into his death?" (Rom 6:3). There is something in our own going down into the waters of baptism and coming up again that gives us insight into Christ's death and resurrection. Notice that he says, "For if we have grown into union with him through a death like his, we shall also be united with him in the resurrection" (Rom 6:5). It is through baptism that we are given our first experience of resurrection. If we want to know about the resurrection of Jesus, we must reflect on our baptism.

The early Church fathers spoke of baptism as a type of resurrection. St. Ambrose said that in going down into the water there is a likeness to death and when you rise there is a likeness to resurrection. This image would perhaps be more real to us if we baptized by immersion. Then, those to be baptized would experience actually going down into the water and coming back up. But if you can picture that happening to you—I mean being thrust under water, feeling desperate for air, and then bursting up, gasping for air—then you begin to get a sense of regeneration, a hint of the new life associated with the resurrection.

I am reminded of the story of the foolish young man who came to a wise, old spiritual master and demanded that he teach him wisdom. The old man took the young man down to the river and held his head under water for a long time. When he finally released him, the young man, sputtering and gasping for air, demanded an explanation for this treatment. The wise spiritual master said, "When you want wisdom as much as you wanted air to breathe just now, come back and see me. I will teach you everything." We must come up out of the waters of baptism desiring God as desperately as a drowning man desires air. This too is an experience of resurrection.

Baptism is a kind of dying. Jesus died in the flesh in order to remove the sin of the world; in baptism, we do not die in the flesh. What dies is our sin, our guilt. So says Cyril of Jerusalem. Freed of guilt, we are able to live, transformed into holiness, a kind of glorious life in the Holy Spirit.

The early writers also speak of remaining dead to sin after baptism. St. John Chrysostom says there are two deaths: one of them accomplished by Christ in baptism and the other by us in remaining dead to sin after our own baptism. We remain dead to sin by our ongoing participation in the life of the Church. In baptism, we surrender ourselves to God. To truly experience resurrection through baptism, the one to be baptized must let go of all self-support, trusting only in the mercy of God. If we are afraid of letting go, of trusting that God will be there, we will not know the full effects of baptism.

I know what it means to be afraid to let go. I grew up on the prairies of North Dakota and never really learned to swim. Thus, I grew up with a kind of nagging fear of water. One day, a good swimmer said to me, "If you want to learn to swim, you must be willing to sink." In other words, if you try by your own effort to stay afloat, you will exhaust yourself. You have to relax, let go, and, then, begin to swim. Is that not also the case with the waters of baptism? Unless you let go, trusting in the mercy of God, you will not learn to swim in the grace-filled world you are entering.

One final story to illustrate this point: A man was alone in a small boat in a large sea when a terrible storm came up. Wind blew, rain came down in torrents, huge waves buffeted the little boat. The man was a Catholic and remembered how Peter had walked on the water. So, he called out, "Lord, Jesus, save me! I am about to drown!" Miraculously, our Lord appeared to him and called to him to leave the boat. The man stepped cautiously out of the boat and made his way to Jesus, where he knelt in gratitude and awe. Jesus looked down at the man and said, "Oh, you of little faith, why are you wearing that life preserver?"

Don't go into the waters of baptism wearing a life preserver! You must come to our Lord with *no* visible means of support. Trust *fully* in the Lord. He has led you to this moment of grace and he will not abandon you. Trust that in the waters of baptism the guilt that weighs you down will be washed away. Then, you will surely rise to walk with our Lord in the joy of Easter.

Questions for Further Discussion:

1. Is the image of baptism as a kind of dying meaningful for you? If not, what image do you prefer?

2. Are you able to let go and swim in the grace-filled waters you are entering? Why or why not?

PART SIX

The Easter Season

HOMILIES 28–37

Lent came out of season
with a fiery baptism
and ashes all over the face of Manhattan,
the dust of poverty and wealth
mingled
in common anguish.

Now the ancient Lenten days
make sacred our pain
shared as we tread the pilgrim road
towards Easter,
for salvation's womb is opened,
by re-membering around a cross
planted
in Ground Zero.

There Christ rises again
from the grave of our securities
and the future pushes green tips
through ashes turned
to soil-made-fertile
by lives laid down for friends,
or even strangers.

And so we dare to whisper,
if not to sing
a gentle
Alleluia.

Sister Bridget Clare McKeever, SSL, "Easter 2002"[1]

28

THE TOMB IS EMPTY!
Easter Sunday (A)

- Acts 10:34a, 37–43
- Colossians 3:1–4
- 1 Corinthians 5:6b–8
- John 20:1–9

The tomb is empty! The tomb in which the body of Jesus was laid on Good Friday, the tomb that had been sealed and even guarded by soldiers, is empty! That is the good news that flashed through heaven and earth, and under the earth, that first Easter Sunday!

Mary Magdala, who came early in the morning looking for Jesus, finds only an empty tomb. Peter and John run to the place where Jesus was laid and what do they find? An empty tomb! The empty tomb is why we are here this morning, why we proclaim: Christ is risen! Indeed, he is truly risen!

It is now some two thousand years since that first morning when the tomb was empty. And as morning breaks on this Easter Sunday, we ponder the same questions the first followers of Jesus pondered: *What does it all mean?* What does it mean for us gathered in this church on this Easter Sunday morning?

Time magazine (April 12, 2004) featured a picture of Jesus on the cover, a noose around his neck, scourged, being led to his death. And the magazine posed this perennial religious question: "Why did Jesus have to die?" As the article notes, Mel Gibson's movie, *The Passion of the Christ,* has brought this question to the fore during Holy Week. *The Passion of the Christ* is a dramatic, although in many ways unhistorical, depiction of what happened to Jesus, but what it does not do is answer the question: *Why?* The *Time* article reprises the various answers given by theologians over the centuries—Christ died as a ransom for our sin, Christ died as a substitute for sinful humanity, Christ died as an example of God's love. Each of these theories is of *some* help, but *none* satisfies completely, because Christ's death and resurrection is part of a great mystery—the paschal mystery. You cannot solve a mystery the way you solve a math problem; you have to embrace the mystery yourself in your own life and thereby come to an intuitive understanding.

To help reach that intuitive understanding, I would suggest a sequel to Mel Gibson's movie. It would be a sequel that would remedy

what I see as the major flaw in *The Passion of the Christ,* the disproportionate focus on the violence of Good Friday at the expense of everything else about the life of Jesus that was redemptive. Such a movie
would seek a fuller understanding of Catholic theology concerning salvation history. This sequel would not be called *Passion II.* No, it would
be called, instead, *Compassion.*

It would be a difficult movie to make, because it would require
the filmmaker to somehow depict the compassion of God. It would
have to show that our God is trinitarian, that the life of the Trinity is
dynamic love, or compassion—compassionate love of the Father for the
Son, Son for the Father, and the expression of that love, the Holy Spirit.

The central theme of this movie, *Compassion,* would be *kenosis,* a
Greek word meaning to empty out. It would open, not with words
from Isaiah, as did *The Passion of the Christ,* but with one of the richest
theological hymns in the Christian scriptures—the second chapter of
the apostle Paul's Letter to the Philippians, read at Mass on Palm
Sunday. These are the words you would hear at the start of the film:

> Christ Jesus, though he was in the form of God,
>> did not regard equality with God
>> something to be grasped.
> Rather, he emptied himself,
>> taking the form of a slave,
>> coming in human likeness;
> and found human in appearance,
>> he humbled himself,
>> becoming obedient to the point of death,
>> even death on a cross.
>
> Because of this, God greatly exalted him
>> and bestowed on him the name
>> which is above every name,
> that at the name of Jesus
>> every knee should bend,
>> of those in heaven and on earth and under the earth,
> and every tongue confess that
>> Jesus Christ is Lord,
>> to the glory of God the Father. (Phil 2:6–11)

The search for an answer to the question, "Why?" must start in the
heart of God, in the life of the Trinity. God *is* compassion, and compassion is what brought God into our world. Christ is the highest
expression of God's compassion. Compassion cannot be contained,

cannot be limited. It had to take up residence in creation, especially in that part of creation made in the image and likeness of God—you and me. That is why we sing in the Exsultet, "O happy fault. O necessary sin of Adam." The story of the empty tomb really begins with the *kenosis* of God: the incarnation, that singular moment in salvation history when Divine Compassion became one with human nature.

It is the nature of God to be emptied out, to be displaced, to seek the lost, to assume the lowest position, to enter into suffering and even death. Why did Jesus have to die? Because God is compassion, ultimate compassion, and compassion cannot stop at half measures. For God, the ultimate form of being emptied out for humankind had to be the sacrifice of the God-man's own life. And that is what Jesus did.

But, of course, what I have said is still not adequate. No movie, no matter how well done, can give us the insight we are seeking. That can only come from living as Christ did. If we live truly compassionate lives, emptying out all the falsehood, all the sin and selfishness that is our human condition, we begin to intuit the meaning of why Christ died. And, what is most important on this Easter Sunday, we begin to sense the meaning of resurrection. When the tombs we sometimes inhabit are emptied, then we rise to live a new life in Christ. That is the glory, the joy, and the hope of this day: What happened to Jesus can and will happen to us.

Questions for Further Discussion:

1. How do you answer the question: Why did Jesus have to die?
2. What does it mean that God is the Divine Compassion?

29
A TALE OF TWO COMMUNITIES
Second Sunday of Easter (A)

- Acts 2:42–47
- 1 Peter 1:3–9
- John 20:19–31

Charles Dickens gave us the classic work, *A Tale of Two Cities*, which begins with the famous line, "It was the best of times; it was the worst of times." The readings today might be called, "A Tale of Two

Communities," for they are about two faith communities that existed in the first century. The readings shed light on our own community, or communities, as we enter the twenty-first century.

The community of faith described in the Acts of the Apostles still basks in the glow of the resurrection. The memory of Christ is fresh; he seems almost present. The apostles are alive and brimming over with faith. It is an ideal Christian community, a community in awe of the signs and wonders performed by the apostles, a community whose numbers were increasing daily.

John's Gospel was written for a much different community. Forty or fifty years have passed since the resurrection. The memory of Christ has begun to fade. Many of the eyewitnesses to the resurrection have died. The signs and wonders have diminished. John's community is in reality two communities—those who knew the Lord firsthand and those who came to believe in the Lord through the testimony of others.

It is for this second community that John tells the famous story of Thomas, the skeptical apostle who needed physical proof of the resurrection. And so the author of John tells of how Jesus appeared to Thomas, how he invited Thomas to touch his resurrected body, and how Thomas, without having touched the Lord, confesses, "My Lord and my God." Then Jesus speaks to Thomas in words that were meant for John's faith community and for us. He says, "Blessed are those who have not seen and have believed" (John 19:29).

These words are meant for us here in our own faith community because, if we think about it, we are much like John's community. We have in our community people whose faith is alive and well; they do not need physical proof in order to believe. We have people whose faith is so strong that the walls of this church could fall down around them and their faith would be unaffected. They would simply pick up the pieces and start rebuilding. We have people who have not seen the Lord and yet have believed all their lives, sometimes fifty, sixty years or more.

But if we think back to last weekend, Easter weekend, we have to admit that there is a second community in every parish—those whose faith is not as strong, those whose faith is fleeting, ephemeral, always on the verge of being submerged in doubt, often overwhelmed by the skepticism of a secular, agnostic world. We saw the members of this second community standing along the sides of the church last weekend or, if they were lucky, crowding into some of our accustomed places in the pews. They are the ones who are not blessed, because they have not seen Christ and find it hard to believe. Fallen-away Catholics, what we jokingly refer to as Christmas & Easter Catholics, are the second largest religious denomination in the United States—surpassed only by the community of believing Catholics.

The question for our faith community at the start of the twenty-first century is no different from the question faced by Christians at the end of the first century—how do we keep faith alive? How do we believe in the Lord when we have not seen him? How do we become one community rather than two?

The issue is a complex one and I do not mean to suggest simple solutions. But I believe a good answer is suggested in the first reading from Acts. What were the early Christians doing to experience Christ as still present among them? The reading from Acts says, "They devoted themselves to the teaching of the apostles and to the communal life, to the breaking of bread and to the prayers" (Acts 2:42). In other words, the early Christians experienced Christ's presence in the liturgy, in the social hour after Mass and regular prayer.

We experience Christ in many ways: in our care for the poor, in our private devotions, in the way we live our daily lives, but the principal way we experience the presence of Christ is through the liturgy. The Church teaches that Christ is present in five ways in the liturgy: Christ is present in the sacrifice of the Mass, not only in the celebrant but especially in the body and blood of Christ; Christ is present in the sacraments—when a minister baptizes, it is really Christ who baptizes; Christ is present when the word is proclaimed—it is Christ himself who speaks when the holy scriptures are read in Church; and finally, Christ is present when the Church prays and sings.

Time does not permit development of all these modes by which Christ is present in the liturgy, so let me focus on the last one—Christ is present when the assembly gathers to pray and sing. When we come together to pray and sing, we do not do so as individuals; we pray and sing as one body. Christ assures us he is present when we gather in his name. But we can do things to enhance the awareness of Christ's presence, especially for those whose faith is weak. We may not always be able to sing like angels, but our awareness of Christ's presence is enhanced when we know the people around us. We pray more fully as one body when we know the needs of the people around us. But how can we know each other's needs if we do not know each other's names?

Why not do something radical today to enhance the awareness of Christ's presence in our assembly as we pray and sing. After the final song, why not introduce yourself to someone you don't know. Or better yet, try something really radical—invite someone you don't know to have coffee with you after Mass.

Sometimes we can be so in awe of the mystery of Christ's presence in the Eucharist that we forget the mystery of Christ's presence in the ordinary things, such as sharing coffee and a doughnut. We need to be reminded, as the first reading from Acts tells us: The early Christians "ate their meals with exultation and sincerity of heart" (Acts 2:46). And in doing that, they experienced Christ present among them.

A small step of common hospitality can be a giant leap toward a greater awareness of Christ's presence. A little kindness can change a "Tale of Two Communities" into a sacred story of *one* community in Christ.

Questions for Further Discussion:

1. Are you aware of another community of Catholics who may find it hard to believe? What do we do to make them more a part of our community?

2. Do you see Christ present in the ordinary things?

30
THEOLOGY IN THE LIFE OF A FRIEND
Third Sunday of Easter (A)

- Acts 2:14, 22–33
- 1 Peter 1:17–21
- Luke 24:13–35

Not long ago, a dear friend of mine, Owen Traynor, died. It was a great honor to me when Owen's wife, Jackie, told me she had found some written instructions Owen had left. Included in those instructions was Owen's request that his good friend, Deacon Mike Bulson, preside and preach at his funeral vigil. And I did. My honoring of Owen's request was a privilege, not just of being a deacon but, more importantly, of being a friend.

The text I chose for the vigil was the Gospel for this Sunday, that beautiful story of the two disciples on the road to Emmaus. The thoughts I expressed at the vigil service apply as well to ourselves on this Third Sunday of Easter. I say that because the Gospel is about encountering the risen Christ on the highways and byways of life. When we share with each other the events of our lives, and especially when we reflect back on the lives of loved ones who have preceded us in death, we are engaging in a form of theological reflection. When done in the light of scripture, such reflection can yield much fruit. My theological reflection on the life of my friend, Owen, is but one example of what I mean.

A few years ago, when Owen and Jackie were celebrating their fiftieth wedding anniversary, their children prepared a unique display to commemorate their parents' years together. It resembled a board game with a long sequence of squares representing the significant events in their life together. The square designated "START" represented the year they met. In the squares that followed, entries were made of births, deaths, job changes, all the events, both happy and sad, they had shared as they walked along the path depicted on the board.

I said to those gathered for the vigil, and I say the same to you here this morning, that in light of the Gospel we just heard, someone else must be represented in each one of those squares on the board. That someone is Christ, the unseen companion on everyone's journey, whether it be to Emmaus, to this church here in Ogden, Utah, or anywhere else that the path of a baptized Christian leads. Christ walked that path unseen because he was hidden in the humanity of Owen, just as he remains disguised in the outward features of every person. Our happy task at a funeral vigil, or at this Sunday Mass, is to find the traces of Christ's presence in the life of everyone who walks the path of life. The disciples on the road to Emmaus found him revealed in the breaking of the bread, just as we do. But if we are attentive, we find him revealed in the life of every person, especially a dear loved one such as Owen.

The Gospel today invites us to theological reflection. By that I mean we sift through the events of our own life, or at a funeral vigil, a loved one's life. We reflect on the stories, the pictures, the relics of a lifetime and, in doing so, come to a more personal understanding of how God is revealed in Jesus. God is revealed in scripture, in nature, and quintessentially in Jesus Christ. Christ is found in the consecrated elements of bread and wine, in the word as it is proclaimed, in the priest at the altar. He is also present in the graced life of each one of us. By becoming aware of that presence we discover a unique revelation of God shining through the life of each person.

At the funeral vigil, I limited myself to three ways in which God was revealed in the life of Owen. What I said then applies equally to each of us. The three ways I noted were love, fidelity, and a sense of humor.

First, about love. You could not be around Owen long without becoming aware of his love for Jackie and his family. I often say to young couples preparing for marriage that their marriage will be a true sacrament if those around them are touched by the love of God pervading their marriage. That was certainly true in Owen's case. His life with Jackie and his family was a true sacrament, for it mediated God's love to those who knew him.

Secondly, I spoke of fidelity. Owen was faithful in all things: faithful in his service to country (joining the navy at age seventeen), faithful to his Catholic beliefs, and faithful to Jackie through fifty-six years of marriage. So faithful was he that he volunteered for an experimental heart pump (LVAD), thereby extending the time he could be with family, despite considerable uncertainty and discomfort.

Finally, Owen revealed some of the humor of God. In his own quiet way he could see the humor in the many twists and turns his life took. That quality of God expressed through the personality of Owen was a delight and comfort for those who knew and cared for him.

It might seem that a board-game depiction of Owen's life, or anyone's life, would have a square at the end designated "FINISH." But, of course, that is not the case. The square really reads "NEW BEGINNING." The path continues, only at a new and more astonishing level.

Questions for Further Discussion:

1. Do you see reflection on your life as a form of theological reflection? How can it benefit you?

2. Do you find Christ revealed in the unique life of every person?

31
MY ARGUMENT WITH THE MAYOR
Fourth Sunday of Easter (A)

- Acts 2:14a, 36–41
- 1 Peter 2:20b–25
- John 10:1–10

I once had a friendly argument with the mayor.

The argument occurred in the context of a monthly meeting of Interfaith Works, a gathering of clergy and lay leaders representing many of the denominations in our community who are committed to social justice. At this particular meeting, the subject of discussion was the future of St. Anne's Center, our local homeless shelter. At issue was whether the city of Ogden would continue to support St. Anne's or whether it intended to push for some alternative for dealing with homelessness. The assertion was made by the mayor and another city representative that the director of St. Anne's had failed in not pushing more vigorously a system of "case management." In other words, every person who came to St. Anne's for food or shelter should be required to participate in programs to achieve self-support and a permanent place to live. The implication was that anyone who did not participate in "case management" should be denied a place to stay.

During the course of the discussion, which became somewhat heated at times with me arguing that all the case management in the world would not wipe out homelessness, someone shouted, "What would Jesus do?" I responded that Jesus would leave the ninety-nine and go in search of the lost sheep. The mayor expressed the opinion that Jesus would not throw the ninety-nine to the wolves while searching for the one lost sheep but would, instead, deal with each on an individual basis. I granted him that, but maintained that my experience as a legal services lawyer for twenty-five years convinced me that a hard core of homeless people would never be benefited by "case management" despite our best intentions. Therefore, we would always need some place where shelter and a meal would be available with no strings attached.

The short dialogue with the mayor is interesting because it shows how the images from today's Gospel are very much a part of our understanding of social justice. In today's Gospel, we are given the image of Jesus the Good Shepherd, tending the sheep, guarding their going and coming, knowing each of them by name, and protecting them from thieves and robbers. The image has its roots in the Old Testament where God was often pictured as the shepherd of the flock.[2] The Book of Ezekiel is especially rich with such images. The image of a shepherd and the shepherding of sheep played a central role in the Hebrew imagination. God is depicted as denouncing those who neglect the sheep who are weak, sick, or straying (Ezek 34:5–6). God, on the other hand, is the faithful shepherd who will lead the sheep "into their own land…and they shall feed on rich pasture on the mountains of Israel" (Ezek 34:13–14 NRSV).

With Jesus, the shepherd imagery received a creative new reinterpretation. The gospels show Jesus as the one in whom God's loving care for the sheep is raised to a new level of meaning. Today's Gospel does support what the mayor was saying about Jesus caring for each sheep individually. After all, to call each sheep by name means Jesus knows them individually. But the level of care certainly goes beyond managing an individual case and sanctioning those who do not comply. Jesus speaks of himself as being the gate for the sheep that will "come in and go out and find pasture." *Pasture* is a word that implies richness, plenty, or fullness of life as the final lines of the Gospel describe. That is what we should be looking for in talking about the homeless and, indeed, about the well-being of all citizens in our community.

Another word we might use to describe the "pasture" of fullness of life we all seek is the Hebrew word, *shalom*. That is the word which should form the ideal of any group of concerned citizens when addressing the issue of homelessness. The biblical understanding of *shalom* is the notion of "well-being or human flourishing and fulfillment…the gift of God rather than something that can be brought about by mere human effort."[3] The richness of *shalom* is expressed in Psalm 85 with these lines:

> Steadfast love and faithfulness will meet,
>   righteousness and peace will kiss each other.
> Faithfulness will spring up from the ground,
>   and righteousness will look down from the sky.
> The LORD will give what is good,
>   and our land will yield its increase.
> Righteousness will go before him,
>   and will make a path for his steps. (Ps 85:10–13 NRSV)

And, again, that same understanding can be heard in these words from Isaiah 65:

> They shall not build and another inhabit;
>   they shall not plant and another eat;
> for like the days of a tree shall the days of my people be,
>   and my chosen shall long enjoy the work of their hands.
>   (Isa 65:22 NRSV)

The kind of community that could truly be called a *shalom*-community does not come without effort and even controversy. While it is a community of peace, it is peace in the biblical sense of justice being done for every member. The effort needed to achieve such a community may at times produce division as members committed to social justice argue with those who may not fully share a vision of *shalom*. And yet, that is what the Gospel calls us to. We now stand in the place of the shepherd described in the Gospel. By his coming into the world, Christ passed to us the shepherd's crook of responsibility for building a community in which all sheep can live in dignity, a community where the sheep can pasture well and enjoy the fullness of life. That is the vocation we are offered by Jesus in the Gospel: to become the shepherds of a flock that cannot always be case-managed into being model sheep. That is our vocation, if we are able to hear the voice of the Good Shepherd calling us to it.

Questions for Further Discussion:

1. Does the image of Jesus as shepherd have meaning for you today?

2. What other images do you find meaningful?

32
ON THE WAY TO A SPECIAL DWELLING PLACE
Fifth Sunday of Easter (A)

- Acts 6:1–7
- 1 Peter 2:4–9
- John 14:1–12

Garrison Keillor, the humorist who has delighted many of us with *A Prairie Home Companion*, is also sometimes a good source for theology. He recently had this to say about religion in Minnesota. He said that Minnesota is such a Lutheran state, even the Catholics are Lutheran. In Minnesota, the Lutherans believe God is Lutheran. He said even the atheists in Minnesota think that if there were a God, that God would be Lutheran.

I was born in Minnesota, and grew up a Lutheran, so I know what Garrison Keillor is talking about. But I have been Catholic all my adult life and I can say that sometimes we may do the same thing—I mean thinking that God is Roman Catholic! Whether we are cradle Catholics or were received into the Church later in life, we may find ourselves thinking, perhaps unconsciously, that we are the chosen ones and it's too bad for the rest of them.

The Franciscan priest, Richard Rohr, calls this "truncated religion." By this he means we have stopped growing in our religious outlook, we have become smug about our "chosenness," we have become well satisfied with who we are and what we are, and we don't see much need for anything further. An extreme example of truncated religion would be the Taliban, or Osama Bin Laden and his followers, who preach a narrow and deadly view of Islam that produces "martyrs" and innocent victims.

But we don't have to go to that extreme example. No matter our religion, we may entertain a secret belief that heaven will be populated mostly by people who believe as we do. You have probably heard that old story of the man who dies and goes to heaven. He is being shown around heaven and, as he walks past one area, St. Peter whispers to him to be quiet. When the man asks why the silence, St. Peter says, "This is where the Catholics live, and they think they're the only ones here." Of course, I have heard that story applied to many other religious denominations. The fact that we are able to laugh at it shows we are aware of our own habits of thinking and don't take ourselves too seriously. However, if I told that story to an Islamic fundamentalist and substituted "Muslim" for Catholic, I would be in trouble.

The point is: It is as silly to think that any particular religious denomination will be the only ones in heaven as it is to think that God is Lutheran. When we realize this, we deepen our appreciation of the mystery of Christ and Christ's saving grace in our world. The grace Christ released into the world through his passion, death, and resurrection cannot be contained. It continues to redeem and transform our world, despite our limitations.

In today's Gospel, our Lord says, "In my Father's house there are many dwelling places. If there were not, would I have told you that I am going to prepare a place for you?" (John 14:2). Why are there "many dwelling places"? Could they not be mansions especially designed for whole communities of believers, both baptized Christians and what the theologian Karl Rahner called "anonymous Christians"? It is possible that the grace of Christ may touch the hearts and minds of people of all races and religions, all nationalities, making it possible for them to share in some way what Christ promises.

Who is the "you" Jesus is referring to? The disciples heard it as meaning themselves. For several years, until St. Paul came along, Peter thought "you" meant those who first became Jews and then were baptized into Christ. Paul said, "No, it includes Gentiles too." Gradually we have come to see that it includes *everybody.* How that will happen is a mystery we cannot penetrate any better than the disciples. We simply believe that Jesus is "the way and the truth and the life" and that no one comes to God, except through Christ. That does not diminish us as Roman Catholics; rather, it *expands* our hope in the saving grace of Christ for the entire world.

The promised "dwelling places" or "mansions" apply not only to other religions, but to our own relationship with God as well. Christ is the Divine Builder who is preparing a dwelling place uniquely suited to each one of us. We cooperate with Christ in preparing a dwelling place for ourselves not just in heaven, but in this life as well. The dimensions of that mansion can also be limited by what we believe and the way we practice our faith. If our image of God, if our thinking about God, if the way we pray to God, has not changed much since childhood, then that dwelling place will never take on the beauty and style God intends for us.

The Divine Builder has an infinite imagination for preparing dwelling places. We must join our imagination with that of Christ as we mutually prepare a place suitable for people made in the image of God. We limit that dwelling place when our imagination has not been fully awakened, when we let our religion become truncated.

But here is the amazing truth about our relationship with God: it *always* has the potential to grow, to renew itself, to bring forth new life. A person's religion may be truncated, but it is *never* dead. It always has the potential of sprouting forth from the roots. Our imagination may fade at times but it can always be reinvigorated.

Our reason for being here today has everything to do with nurturing our religion, making it grow and produce fruit we may have never imagined possible. Through the sacraments, our prayer, our study, our service to others, we revive and nurture our religious life. We enhance our imagination for what is possible in Christ.

Our God is not Lutheran. Our God is not Roman Catholic. Our God is the God of *all* creation. Our way to God is through Christ, the way and the truth and the life.

Questions for Further Discussion:

1. Have you ever thought of God as favoring one denomination over another?

2. Do you believe it is possible for persons who do not believe in Christ, or perhaps ever heard of him, to be saved?

33

WHOM TO EXCLUDE FROM A DAY OF PRAYER
Sixth Sunday of Easter (A)

- Acts 8:5–8, 14–17
- 1 Peter 3:15–18
- John 14:15–21

Recently, while looking through some newspaper clippings on the National Day of Prayer, I was reminded of how far we have to go before the words of Jesus in today's Gospel are realized. Jesus spoke of a day to come when "you will realize that I am in my Father and you are in me and I in you." This beautiful trinitarian statement apparently had no effect on the people organizing the prayer day.

According to the newspaper account, the National Day of Prayer was established by Congress in 1952. In 1988, it was amended to designate the day as the first Thursday in May. What caught my attention was the fact that the National Day of Prayer Task Force chose to *exclude* members of the Church of Jesus Christ of Latter-day Saints (LDS)—also known as Mormons—from participating in the National Day of Prayer. One reason given by a task force spokesman for the exclusion was that the Mormon faith is not in accordance with the evangelical principles of the group, including its belief in the Holy Trinity.[4] The unnuanced explanation offered by our local newspaper was that the National Day of Prayer Task Force believes "that the Father, the Son and the Holy Spirit are all one being. The Mormon church believes they are distinct."[5]

I suppose if you want to find some reason for excluding the majority of people in Utah from a National Day of Prayer, the task force's insistence on theological purity is one way of doing it. On the other hand, given the crises our nation faces at home and abroad, you would think the group would want to include every person of good will capable of praying in the name of whatever Source of holiness he or she finds meaningful. I wanted to say to the folks on the task force that we Catholics have struggled for centuries to articulate our belief about the Trinity and, while we have never been able to do so adequately, we are at least wise enough to know better than to exclude from prayer those who have a different formulation of the mystery.

We probably cannot do much to change the thinking of the task force. So what can we as Catholics do to avoid falling into the same trap? How do we realize in ourselves the reality that Jesus is in the Father, we in him, and he in us. In other words, how do we actualize what we dimly perceive—that we are all one in Christ and in the love of the Trinity, regardless of our inability to articulate that belief? Mindful of St. Peter's counsel in the second reading, how do we give a reason for our hope in Christ, and do it "with gentleness and reverence"?

It is clear from the scripture readings today that the key to all this is the Holy Spirit. When the events recorded in the first reading from Acts took place, Jews probably had attitudes toward anyone from Samaria that were as divisive as those held by the National Day of Prayer Task Force. And yet, Acts records that Philip, himself a Jew, went to the city of Samaria and worked great signs among the people. He was followed by Peter and John, who prayed with the new converts, "laid hands on them and they received the Holy Spirit." Just a few weeks ago, we heard in the passion accounts of how divisive Peter could be, even to the point of drawing a sword to cut off a man's ear. Today, he speaks of "gentleness and reverence," of suffering for good, and of how Christ was "brought to life in the Spirit. "

The first two readings today are vivid testimony that those who truly love Jesus and keep his commandments will not be left orphans but will be enlivened and enlightened by the Holy Spirit. This is not something that happens easily or automatically. The mere appending of the designation "Christian" to ourselves, the wearing of a cross around the neck, or a fish symbol on the back of our car, does not guarantee that the Spirit of truth will be revealed to us. Jesus says in the Gospel that the Spirit will be revealed to those who love Jesus and keep his commandments. To love someone, you must first know that person. We come to know Jesus the way we come to know any person: by spending quality time with him or her. We come to love Jesus by studying and meditating on scripture, by prayer, and by imitating his words and ways in our life. The same is true with his commandments that were condensed to two: Love God with all your heart, mind, and soul; and love your neighbor as yourself. It is through faithful devotion to these commandments that the Spirit is revealed to us.

When the Spirit is revealed to us, we have the humility to recognize that no one has a monopoly on deciding who is acceptable to God, or who can pray to God in public for the good of our country. It is tempting in a state like our own beloved Utah, with its pervasive Mormon influence, to lapse into an "us-against-them" mentality. We see this in some of the offensive protests made by self-declared Christian evangelists in front of the Mormon temple, and we see it when Mormons are excluded from "Christian" prayer events. But is this loving Jesus and his commandments? I think not.

Another newspaper article reporting on the National Day of Prayer that took place in Ogden included a quote from one organizer of the event who noted how "some religious leaders may find it difficult to pray out loud outdoors."[6] He added, "I don't see Catholic priests or Mormon bishops praying at the corner." I cannot speak for Catholic priests, but as a deacon I would not be comfortable praying with any group that excluded the majority of Utahns, be they Mormons, Unitarians, Jews, or even pagans, for that matter.

The business of excluding people is really a diversion that keeps the unsuspecting from coming to a real awareness of the unity that already exists among us, albeit at a much deeper level. By using their own limited understanding of the Holy Trinity as a shibboleth for deciding who is worthy to pray for the nation, the task force organizers were participating in a myth-building exercise designed to confirm them in their own self-constructed unreality. Such an exercise can be satisfying to some. But the danger of such exercises is that they keep well-meaning people from realizing that we are all one in Christ and live now in the life of the Trinity, despite our inability to articulate that truth adequately. By loving Jesus and keeping his commandments, in particular, his new commandment that we love one another, we hasten the day when the light of the Spirit will reveal that we all pray as one to God the Father. When that happens, a National Day of Prayer will be truly meaningful.

Questions for Further Discussion:

1. Do you think there are any legitimate reasons for excluding a group from a National Day of Prayer? What might they be?

2. How do we give witness to our hope in Christ and do it with gentleness and reverence?

34
THE ASCENSION PARADOX
Ascension of the Lord (A)

- Acts 1:1–11
- Ephesians 1:17–23
- Matthew 28:16–20

St. Bernard of Clairvaux, one of the great religious figures of the twelfth century, once made a very interesting statement about the ascension of the Lord. In one of his many sermons preached on the ascension, he made this paradoxical statement about Christ: "It is in his very descending that he ascended."[7] Bernard was saying something quite akin to what Paul wrote in Ephesians, where he says of Christ, "He who descended is the same one who ascended far above all the heavens, so that he might fill all things" (Eph 4:10 NRSV).

What was it, then, that we find in both Christ's descending—the incarnation—and his ascending—the ascension? Bernard says it is *humility*. Bernard's use of paradox is indeed apt, for we believe that it was by humbling himself, even to accepting death on a cross, as Paul says in Philippians, that Christ was "lifted up" into heaven. It was Christ's loving humility that first brought him among us and the same loving humility that took him from us. That is what we believe and celebrate on this feast day.

What should come to mind when we contemplate the mystery of the ascension is humility: Christ's humility and our own. There is something in the ascension of Christ that we must desire and seek in ourselves. One author reflecting on Bernard's sermon says simply, "A person rises only by humility."[8] By *rise* he, of course, does not mean going up into the clouds. We are not talking about levitation. What is meant is to rise above all that keeps us from being united with God, whether we speak of it as sin, ignorance, or simply our human condition, weighing us down, denying us true freedom.

St. John Cassian says somewhere that, in its natural state, our soul is like a feather that rises, floating easily on the breeze. But it becomes heavy with the weight of cares and concerns, the way a feather becomes damp with moisture and will no longer rise. Humility is what restores us to that natural state of lightness.

What, then, do we mean by humility? Like so many things in the life of the spirit, *humility* is a word that can be easily misunderstood.

One early source I have found helpful on this subject is a little-known bishop of the early Church, St. Diadochos of Photiki, who lived between 400 and 486 in northern Greece. In his book, *Spiritual Knowledge and Discrimination,* which makes up part of the spiritual classic, *The Philokalia,* he says bluntly, "Humility is hard to acquire, and the deeper it is, the greater the struggle needed to gain it."[9] He distinguishes between two types of humility. First, St. Diadochos says there is the humility that comes from bodily weakness and from the actions of people "gratuitously hostile to those pursuing righteousness." This type of humility is experienced during the first stage of our spiritual growth and, though necessary, is only a precursor to real humility. Perhaps we have had some experience of this kind of humility when we have been put down, mistreated, or abused, and have been unable to do much about it. Life experiences of this kind produce a kind of humility but not the ideal, for such humility, according to Diadochos, is usually marked by "remorse and despondency," feelings which do not make for the lightness of a feather.

The second kind of humility that St. Diadochos would want to find in all of us he describes as a divine blessedness. Of this type of humility, he says, "But when the intellect fully and consciously senses the illumination of God's grace, the soul possesses a humility which is, as it were, natural."[10] This is a fascinating observation, for it seems to say that humility is part of our natural makeup. That would go along with what Cassian said about how, in our natural state, our souls rise like feathers. We arrive at this stage of humility by allowing grace to act on our human nature, restoring it to what it was before the taint of original sin affected us.

In calling this humility "divine blessedness," Diadochos is telling us it is gift. Strangely, he says we *cannot* receive the gift of this second kind of humility without passing through the first stage where we are buffeted by all the forces of life that in some way humble us. But it is the second kind of humility that enables us to rise—and it is pure gift. Like all gifts it *cannot* be forced. It has to be waited upon patiently. But perhaps it is by accepting the things we cannot change, not with resignation or remorse, but by combining them with prayer, fasting, and every other good spiritual practice, that we coax into existence the great gift of true humility. We know that we have this gift, Diadochos says, when our experience is marked by "joy and enlightened reverence. "

I suppose the reason most of us spend so much of our lives experiencing humility of the first kind, and not humility as gift, is that we neglect to ask God for the divine blessedness. We forget that God is infinitely generous and will give us *any* spiritual gift we sincerely desire and ask for. The hope on this feast day is that we will be filled by the grace Christ gave us by his descending and ascending. With that grace, may we hasten the day when our lives will be marked by the joy and reverence of true humility. On that day, we will truly rise.

Questions for Further Discussion:

1.How important is humility in your spiritual life? How do you achieve it?

2.Do you agree that we ascend by our humility? What does that mean to you?

35
LAST WORDS
Seventh Sunday of Easter (A)

- Acts 1:12–14
- 1 Peter 4:13–16
- John 17:1–11a

We attach great significance to a person's last words, especially if that person has lived a notable life. Last words spoken as death approaches often afford a final insight into the essence of a person's life: what was important to him or her. Sometimes those last words can inspire us to emulate whatever was great or heroic in that person.

As Robert E. Lee, the much-revered general of the Confederacy, lay dying, he seemed prepared to fight yet another battle, for he ordered General A. P. Hill to bring up his troops just as he had done in previous battles. Then, he spoke his final words: "Strike the tent." The great French philosopher of the Enlightenment, Voltaire, when asked on his deathbed to renounce the Devil, reportedly said, "This is no time for making new enemies."[11] And the words attributed to Thoreau on his deathbed bespeak the soul of a man at peace with the world. When someone asked Thoreau whether he had made his peace with God, he replied: "We have never quarreled." Others might mention Oscar Wilde saying, "Either that wallpaper goes, or I go." And finally, the great Goethe: "More Light! MORE LIGHT!"

In today's Gospel, the start of the seventeenth chapter of John, we hear some of the last words Jesus would speak before his death at Calvary. They too express the essence of Jesus' life. His life, as we know from the gospels, was lived in union with God the Father. His last words reflect that same union, for they are a high priestly prayer, a kind of intimate family conversation. They are not a prayer of intercession but of revelation. Today's Gospel is one not so much to be proclaimed and broken open through preaching as it is one to be listened to reverently, to be meditated on and internalized. If we listen carefully, we begin to realize that we are hearing something divine. It is as though Jesus has already ascended to the Father. His prayer reveals that intimate relationship between Son and Father that John tells us existed from the beginning. If we can penetrate the depths of this prayer, we discover the essence of Jesus' life.

The key to grasping the meaning of this prayer is the word *glory*. Scholars tell us that John's theme throughout the latter chapters of his Gospel is glory. Indeed, Jesus begins with the words, "[G]lorify your Son so that the Son may glorify you" (John 17:1 NRSV). But how are we to understand the word *glory*, a word we ordinarily use to mean exalted praise, honor, or distinction bestowed on someone, for example, to win glory on the battlefield? In the context of Jesus' life as John presents it, glory has more to do with eternal life. Jesus gives glory to God the Father by bringing eternal life to those who came to believe in him. We in turn add to the glory of God by accepting that gift and by living fully the eternal life Jesus brought to the world.

The last words of Jesus should evoke in us a deeper awareness of being fully alive. Our entering into eternal life gives glory to God the Father when we see this gift as more than something reserved for life after death. The glory of eternal life is right now, if we can realize it. How to do that? We do that by being completely open to the light, truth, and joy inherent in the Gospel. When these aspects of eternal life are fully present in us, then God is glorified. When the words of Jesus, which have reached their pinnacle in this prayer, have entered our being, then death is overcome. Then, we no longer are bound but are freed to live life in its fullness.

We have the last words of many famous people. But we do not have the last words of any of those who heard Jesus' prayer to his

Father. What were the last words of Peter, of John, James, of Mary and the other women mentioned in the first reading from Acts? We do not know but we do know that they were "constantly devoting themselves to prayer." It is, I think, safe to infer from this that their last words would have been reflective of the lives they lived. Their last words must have borne witness to the reality that Jesus had been glorified in them.

And how about *us*? Do our lives reveal that Jesus has been glorified in us? And will our last words be reflective of our lives in Christ?

There is an old and venerable tradition in our Church of practicing mindfulness of death. Best expressed in St. Benedict's words, *memento mori*, this tradition has lost some of its value in our death-denying culture. Perhaps one way of revitalizing that tradition would be to develop a practice of asking ourselves what we would like our last words to be. What would you want your final words to be? What will they tell the survivors about your own life? Will they reflect the essence of your life? Will they reveal that you entered into eternal life long before you died? May the Eucharist we are about to share bring us to that eternal life.

Questions for Further Discussion:

1. Do a person's last words reveal something about that person?
2. What would you want *your* last words to be?

36
ZENTECOST
Pentecost Vigil

> • Genesis 11:1–9
> • Romans 8:22–27
> • John 7:37–39

"In the beginner's mind there are many possibilities, but in the expert's mind there are few." Shunryu Suzuki[12]

Pentecost is traditionally thought of as the beginning of the Church. Looking back over two-thousand years, many of us could give a general account of that history, could talk about the major events, perhaps summarize many of the doctrines and dogma that have been handed down to us. We are all experts in the sense that we have a lot more crammed into our heads than did those early followers of Jesus who first experienced Pentecost. We have experts in theology, in liturgy, in Church history, canon law. But as the quote from Suzuki tells us, being an expert comes at a price. We may have *limited* the possibilities.

On this Pentecost Vigil, I invite you to step back and try to regain a Catholic beginner's mind with all the possibilities that entails. I invite you to return to the beginner's mind of the Church. But I must warn you: It will not be easy. The best analogy for what I am proposing comes from the Zen Buddhist tradition where the Zen masters emphasize the importance of "beginner's mind," that form of consciousness which lies hidden beneath all the accretions of human experience, and which must be awakened if enlightenment is to occur. I think that the experience of the first Christians at Pentecost had a Zen-like quality of beginner's mind. Their encounter with the Spirit of God was direct, immediate, and as yet uncluttered by creeds, councils or canons. The descent of the Holy Spirit on the apostles was like a Zen master's slap to the face of a student, shocking him into enlightenment. In many ways we have lost the ability to have that direct experience. Our consciousness, so clouded with centuries of necessary but sometimes deadening formulations, awaits the slap of a master to bring it into true awareness of God.

Let me be clear: I am *not* preaching a kind of anti-intellectualism here. I am *not* advocating that we get rid of creeds or even the code of canon law. All the canons, rules, doctrines, and dogma that occupy our minds as Church members serve an important—a very important—purpose. We live in a sinful world and we contend with an adversary who does not acquiesce. Living out the gospel, especially its moral teachings, *requires* that we be experts at times. But there is a time for all things. And tonight is the time to return to a Catholic beginner's mind. Tonight is the time to put on a mind that is open to all possibilities.

What are the possibilities? There is the real possibility of having a direct and immediate experience of the Holy Spirit! I think perhaps the greatest scandal of our modern Catholic age is that so many believers have pretty much written off that possibility. For many, I am afraid, church life is still more about obligation, habit, perhaps even superstition. Far too many have not felt the Holy Spirit's slap to the cheek that brings enlightenment. And yet there are still those among us with beginner's minds, those who know that when the Spirit comes, something wonderful and marvelous is possible. It is possible, as our Lord says, that "[r]ivers of living water will flow from within him who believes in me" (John 7:38).

There is the possibility of an experience of real freedom. That is what a beginner's mind knows—*freedom*. Zen teaches that we are born "free and equal." It is only gradually over time that we accumulate all the baggage that keeps us from experiencing our original freedom. Everything that a Zen master does, all the physical and mental exercises, is intended to restore the student to that original state of freedom. We should not find this strange, for, indeed, Jesus said in the Gospel, "Truly I tell you, whoever does not receive the kingdom of God as a little child will never enter it" (Mark 10:15 NRSV). A child's mind is a beginner's mind.

The path a student of Zen must follow to retrieve that beginner's mind is a great struggle, for the masters know the extent of mental inertia that has to be overcome. Jesus knew the same, for he spoke of the Kingdom of God as being as difficult to enter as a camel passing through the eye of a needle (Mark 10:25). There is a kind of Catholic inertia that can take over in our spiritual lives as well. We can become so complacent, so accustomed to the customary, that we are unable to find joy in the freshness of the Holy Spirit. It takes a rigorous struggle, such as one finds in Zen, to awaken in ourselves an awareness of reality, of what truly matters. But when that awareness happens, we throw out the living room furniture, as the Zen people say. Or, as Jesus once said, we sell all that we have and purchase the pearl of great price.

The effort I am suggesting that is necessary to regain a beginner's mind may *not* be for everyone. I acknowledge the criticism that such rigors should be preached only to the "elite" and not to "ordinary" Christians. Still, I am reluctant to make that concession. The sacrifice demanded is worth it. It is worth it because of the possibilities.

Questions for Further Discussion:

1. Have you experienced in yourself what is referred to as "beginner's mind"? Is it possible? Desirable?

2. How do you experience the Holy Spirit in your life?

37
HOLY SPIRIT: BREATH OF LIFE
Pentecost (A)

> • Acts 2:1–11
> • 1 Corinthians 12:3b–7, 12–13
> • John 20:19–23

Many images come to mind when we think of the Holy Spirit: tongues of fire, a mighty wind, a dove. But in today's Gospel on this feast of Pentecost, we are given a very intimate image. The Gospel says that Jesus breathed on the disciples and said, "Receive the Holy Spirit." The Holy Spirit is the breath of God. It is the breath of God that creates, gives life, purifies, and sanctifies. What a marvelous image of God's divine action in us!

This is not the only place that scripture speaks of the breath of God. Remember the second creation account in the second chapter of Genesis? The author of Genesis describes the creation of humankind in this way: "[T]hen the Lord God formed man from the dust of the ground, and breathed into his nostrils the breath of life; and the man became a living being" (Gen 2:7 NRSV). No other form of creation mentioned in Genesis is given the "breath" of life. Only humankind is singled out for this divine gift. Our race received its first breath of life from God at the dawn of creation; it received its second breath of life at Pentecost. We believe that divine breath to be the Holy Spirit.

Down through the centuries, from creation to Pentecost, inspired persons—Job, the psalmist, Ezekiel—*all* testified to the presence of God's life-giving breath. Thus, Job declares: "In his hand is the life of every living thing and the breath of every human being" (Job 12:10 NRSV). And, again, "The spirit of God has made me, and the breath of the Almighty gives me life" (Job 33:4 NRSV). The psalmist too takes up this theme: "By the word of the Lord the heavens were made, and all their host by the breath of his mouth" (Ps 33:6 NRSV). Finally, when the prophet Ezekiel was told to prophesy over the dry bones, the Lord directed, "Prophesy to these bones, and say to them: O dry bones, hear the word of the Lord. Thus says the Lord God to these bones: I will cause breath to enter you, and you shall live. I will lay sinews on you, and will cause flesh to come upon you, and cover your skin, and put breath in you, and you shall live; and you shall know that I am the Lord" (Ezek 37:4–6 NRSV).

The divine breath that gives life, even to dry bones, has not been withheld from God's chosen people. Recently, I watched a PBS special about the great Jewish psychiatrist, Victor Frankl, who survived Auschwitz and wrote a number of excellent books. Victor Frankl learned something very important from his death-camp experience. He learned that those who survived were those who found meaning in their lives. Frankl identified two main sources of meaning: work and love. Those who can work and love, which includes most of us, are able to find meaning. Love especially is capable of giving meaning. If we are able to love someone, if we are able to transcend our own selfish interests and care for another deeply, even passionately, over a long time, we are blessed with meaning.

What Victor Frankl learned in a concentration camp, and wrote about so convincingly, has been a breath of life for many. I myself found his early work, *Man's Search for Meaning*, an important part of my own formation as a young adult. And when I grow tired of giving myself wholly to others in my work or in my ministry, I remember this story Victor Frankl tells.

It happened once that Victor Frankl, while practicing psychiatry in New York, received a very late phone call from a woman who was ready to commit suicide. Frankl spent an hour, using his best arguments from his study and practice of psychiatry to convince her not to take her own life. Several days later the woman came to Frankl's office and he was overjoyed to see that she was still alive. He asked the woman which of his arguments had persuaded her not to end her life. The woman replied that it was none of the learned arguments that convinced her; what convinced her, she said, was that a very busy and important psychiatrist would spend an hour in the middle of the night talking to her. That was what kept her alive. Victor Frankl had given her the breath of life.

Today, we need that breath of life more than ever. As I follow the news I am reminded again and again of how desperate is the search for meaning among so many people in our world. Millions of dollars are spent, millions of miles are traveled, all in desperate search for something—entertainment, fashion, technology, drugs, pornography—something—anything—that will satisfy, something to give meaning. And all the time, meaning is waiting for those who work and love. Those who are able to accept and apply this truth in their life have truly received the breath of life.

On this feast when we celebrate the coming of the Holy Spirit among us, I invite you to ask: Where is the breath of life, the breath of

God, experienced in my life? Do you experience it here at Mass? I hope so. Do you feel it when you are in loving relationship with another? And do you feel that breath of life fade away when you rupture a relationship? You should, because that is where the breath of life is most real: in loving relationships. When it is allowed to dissipate, we become like dry bones, waiting for a prophet to call down the breath of life on us.

My friends, receive the breath of life again today! Receive the Holy Spirit!

Questions for Further Discussion:

1. Where is the breath of life experienced in your life?
2. Do you agree that work and love make life meaningful?

PART SEVEN

Ordinary Time

HOMILIES 38–67

The joys and the hopes, the griefs and the anxieties of the men of
this age, especially those who are poor or in any way afflicted, these
too are the joys and hopes, the griefs and anxieties of the followers
of Christ. Indeed, nothing genuinely human fails to raise an echo in
their hearts. For theirs is a community composed of men.
United in Christ, they are led by the Holy Spirit in their journey
to the kingdom of their Father and they have welcomed the news
of salvation which is meant for every man. That is why this
community realizes that it is truly and intimately
linked with mankind and its history.

From the preface to *Gaudium et spes,* the Pastoral Constitution
on the Church in the Modern World[1]

38

TRINITARIAN FOOTPRINTS
Holy Trinity Sunday (A)

- Exodus 34:4b–6, 8–9
- 2 Corinthians 13:11–13
- John 3:16–18

We have all probably heard that little story often called "Footprints in the Sand." As the story goes, a man is shown an image of his life in the form of footprints traced in the sand. He sees two sets of footprints and is told by Jesus that the footprints represent the man's path through life, with one set of prints being the man's and the other that of Jesus. When he comes to a time in his life when he went through great adversity, the man notes that there is only one set of prints and he asks our Lord why he abandoned him. Jesus explains that during that period of time, the man's footprints were absent because Jesus was carrying him. Other variations on this story mention footprints that indicate times when the man danced with Jesus on the shore.

Today, on this feast of the Trinity, I want to borrow this same image of footprints in the sand to suggest another way of approaching this great mystery. If we are attentive, we may be able to spot footprints of the Holy Trinity in our lives. They are the footprints of the Father, the Son, and the Holy Spirit. At times the footprints of each appear distinct but, in truth, they are one.

The great Jesuit theologian, Karl Rahner, says in his book, *Foundations of Christian Faith,*[2] that the mystery of the Trinity is largely incomprehensible to people today. The explanation of the Trinity as three distinct Persons with one nature fails to register any real meaning with contemporary Christians who are accustomed to thinking of *person* as meaning the same as when the word is used in other contexts. Such traditional metaphors as the shamrock do little to overcome this obstacle. In trying to understand the life of the Trinity, Rahner says that a psychological model, which speaks of the Father loving himself in the Son, the Son reciprocating that love, and the Holy Spirit as the fruit of that love, is also inadequate. In place of such approaches, Rahner suggests that we look for the "immanent" Trinity in the "economy of salvation" itself. In other words, we find the footprints of the Trinity "in both the collective and individual history of salvation."[3]

Karl Rahner summarizes this approach as follows:

> Insofar as he has come as the salvation which divinizes us in the innermost center of the existence of the individual person, we call him really and truly "Holy Spirit" or "Holy Ghost." Insofar as in the concrete historicity of our existence one and the same God strictly as himself is present for us in Jesus Christ, and in himself, not in a representation, we call him "Logos" or the Son in an absolute sense. Insofar as this very God, who comes to us as Spirit and as Logos, is and always remains the ineffable and holy mystery, the incomprehensible ground and origin of his coming in the Son and in the Spirit, we call him the one God, the Father.[4]

With this wonderfully concise statement from Karl Rahner as our starting point, let us look for footprints of the Trinity.

Divinization is not a word we hear much these days but that is the word Rahner and others use to describe the activity of the Holy Spirit in our lives. Some of the early Church fathers liked to say that God became human so that humankind might become God. In other words, the footprints of the Holy Spirit tell us of God's grace at work in our nature making us holy and like God—not becoming God, but becoming *like* God in holiness. When we are aware of spiritual growth in our lives, when we sense a deeper holiness, when we feel ourselves moving "from glory to glory," then we have detected the footprints of the Holy Spirit. We are helped in our growing awareness by good habits of prayer, confession and reconciliation, and true remorse for our sinfulness.

At times we are also aware of the presence of Christ among us. Perhaps in prayer, in meditation, in reading the scriptures, and in the Eucharist, we discover in ourselves and those around us that the Son-Logos has, indeed, taken on our nature. The Church tries to help us to heighten that awareness through the liturgical seasons as we move from the incarnation, through ordinary time, Easter, and again through ordinary time. We cooperate with what is offered us by a full, conscious participation during the Mass and by continuing the sacrifice of the Mass by the way we live after we are dismissed. One of the surest signs that we have expanded our capacity to recognize the footprints of the Son in our lives is when we see the poor and the disadvantaged as Christ in disguise. Then, with the help of the Holy Spirit, we do all that we can to bring about social justice wherever we are capable of making a difference.

Finally, while we are being divinized by the Holy Spirit and are becoming more united with Christ in his many forms, we grow in reverence for the great mystery of God the Father, the creator of all things who has formed us in the divine image. We may find ourselves marveling in mystical awe at the delicate and intricate mystery of nature. We may stand in silence before a God who made the Pleiades and Orion, who set the planets on their course and who created you and me just less than angels. We may catch an intuitive glimpse of God the Father at work in human history as we study the books of the Bible, both old and new. And we rejoice with the Church in knowing the Son, the ultimate revelation of God the Father.

At the risk of leaning too heavily on the footprints metaphor, we might think of our experience of the Trinity as an amazing depiction of the divine dance, the *perichoresis*, taking place in the history of the world, of which our individual lives are a part. We may picture those footprints going on through all time and eternity, with our own unique prints mysteriously interwoven in the pattern. So, let us continue the dance!

Questions for Further Discussion:

1. Can you detect the footprints of the Trinity in your life? What do they tell you?

2. Are there other images of the Trinity that you find more meaningful?

39

COME, TASTE THE FINE FOOD AND ENJOY
Body and Blood of Christ

- Deuteronomy 8:2–3, 14b–16a
- 1 Corinthians 10:16–17
- John 6:51–58

Imagine that you are invited to a fabulous dinner, and you say, "I will go, but I will not enjoy it."

Imagine that the dinner is to be prepared by the most famous chef in the world, who will serve a seven-course dinner of the finest foods and excellent wines, and you say, "I will taste the food, but I will not enjoy it."

Imagine that you go to this fine dinner and you say nothing about the excellent food but only talk about the weather.

This is a scene from the Academy Award-winning film, *Babette's Feast,* a film with rich Eucharistic imagery for this feast of the Body and Blood of Christ.

Babette's Feast is set in a Scandinavian country in the latter part of the 1800s. The village is near the coast and is depicted as cold, windswept, and often quite bleak. In the village there is an old Lutheran minister who has faithfully shepherded his small flock for many years. He is a deeply religious man, loved and admired by his followers. Being a good Lutheran, the minister named his two daughters Martina, after Martin Luther, and Phillipa, after Luther's supporter, Phillip Melancthon.

Time goes by and both Martina and Phillipa miss chances to marry. After the beloved Lutheran minister dies, the daughters try to carry on their father's ministry by gathering the flock to sing the old songs, to repeat the minister's words, and to care for the sick. But gradually the flock begins to drift apart. They remember old grievances, they quarrel among themselves, and their once warm and friendly relationships now become as frigid as the Scandinavian winter.

But then something unexpected happens. A young French woman, named Babette, arrives from France to live with Martina and Phillipa and begins working for them as housekeeper and cook. Dutifully, she learns how to cook the dry lean fish and to make a kind of soup from hard bread that the villagers are accustomed to. For many years she works this way as the little church becomes more and more divided.

Then something unexpected happens again: Babette wins the French lottery. Martina and Phillipa fear that she will leave them and return to Paris but, instead, Babette announces that she wants to use the money to prepare a dinner to celebrate the birthday of Martina and Phillipa's father, the beloved old Lutheran minister.

The daughters cannot say no, nor can the members of the little church. But when they hear about the rich food and fine wine Babette is planning, their reaction is that it would be sinful to take pleasure in such fine food. They resolve that they will *taste* the food, but will *not* enjoy it.

Then comes the night of the great feast. The small flock of aging villagers, clad in their dark, heavy clothing, arrives and is seated at a beautifully set table, with fine china and crystal. They are served the finest, choicest wines from France, rich turtle soup, and finally the *pièce de résistance—caille en sarchophage*—baked quail in little pastry shells. At first, the guests silently repeat their resolution: We will taste the food but not enjoy it; but gradually the food and drink begin to have their effect. A marvelous transformation begins to take place. Men who before were quarreling over an old grievance now are joking about it. People who had become distant and separated from each other now begin to smile at each other, to greet and bless one another. They recall the old minister's sayings and some of the seemingly miraculous things he did. By the time the fresh fruit, rich dessert, and coffee arrive, the people are singing and embracing. Through Babette's feast, forgiveness and reconciliation have taken place.

I wonder if perhaps sometimes we are like the alienated Scandinavians who came to Babette's feast with a subtle predisposition to not enjoy it. If we come to this feast of the Body and Blood of Christ still compelled by a sense of obligation instilled in us during our youth, then maybe we do not want to really enjoy it. If we come out of a sense of fear, thinking that if we don't come something bad will happen to us, then we are in a sense saying, "I will eat but I will not enjoy it."

And yet I have noticed in myself, and perhaps you have experienced it too, that coming to the Eucharist, participating in the liturgy, and receiving the body and blood of Christ has a transforming effect, regardless of what brought me there. If we come to the table of the Lord expecting divine nourishment, expecting we will enjoy the feast, then our attitude begins to change. The reconciliation that Babette's guests experienced is a natural effect of sharing food and drink. But it points to something even more satisfying—the reconciliation with God and neighbor on a supernatural level offered to those who partake as one body in the body and blood of Christ.

Forgiveness and reconciliation do not happen in a vacuum. They need the mediation of ordinary things, such as a fine feast prepared by a French chef. Forgiveness and reconciliation are mediated by our actions, both during and after the Eucharist, by our prayerfulness and active participation in the liturgy. But also by such ordinary things as joining in a Mexican breakfast served after Mass, by the sharing of coffee and doughnuts with someone we don't know, by small communities of faith who share faith together. All of these create opportunities for reconciliation.

Our Lord, like a fine French chef, has prepared a feast for us from his own body and blood. What an insult to the chef if we come with an attitude of "I will taste but not enjoy." Or worse, if we decide not to come at all. God's mercy is infinite. Despite our turning away, God will prepare this great feast throughout all of time. Every Eucharist, God will offer us "a feast of rich food, a feast of well-aged wines, of rich food filled with marrow, of well-aged wines strained clear" (Isa 25:6 NRSV).

One of the guests at Babette's feast is an old general who, as a young officer had fallen in love with Martina, only to reject her for a military career in France. As the dinner reaches its conclusion, he stands, lifts his glass and speaks these words:

> Mercy and truth have met together
> Righteousness and bliss shall kiss one another.
> Man in his weakness and shortsightedness
> Believes he must make choices in this life.
> He trembles at the risk he takes.
> We do know fear,
> But, lo,
> Our choice is of no importance.
> There comes a time when your eyes are opened
> And we come to realize that mercy is infinite.
> We need only await it with confidence
> And receive it in gratitude.
> Mercy imposes no conditions
> And lo,
> Everything we have chosen has been given to us.
> And everything we rejected has also been granted.
> Yes, we even get back what we rejected.
> For mercy and truth are met together
> And righteousness and bliss shall kiss one another.

My friends, come to the feast. Come to the Eucharist.
Come and taste and enjoy. Receive the body and blood of Christ.
Come and receive forgiveness and be reconciled.
Come to the great feast of the Lord.

Questions for Further Discussion:

1. Can you see in Babette's feast images of our own eucharistic celebration? What are the common elements?

2. What keeps us from fully tasting and enjoying the feast?

40
COME AND GO
Tenth Sunday in Ordinary Time (A)

- Hosea 6:3–6
- Romans 4:18–25
- Matthew 9:9–13

Being a disciple of Jesus can be expressed in two little words, words we learned at an early age, words we scratched out on a piece of wide-lined paper in first grade. The words are *come* and *go*.

Mark's Gospel records Jesus walking along the Sea of Galilee, where he sees Simon and Andrew fishing, and we hear: "Follow me and I will make you fish for people" (Mark 1:17 NRSV). In John's Gospel, two disciples ask Jesus where he is staying and he responds simply, "Come and see" (John 1:39 NRSV). And today we hear the call of Matthew: "Follow me," with the little word *come* being implicit in Jesus' invitation.

And it is an *invitation, not* a *command*. The call to a deeper relationship with Jesus is *always* by invitation. Like a gracious host, Jesus extends a welcoming hand, trusting that there will be a response. The first word is always *come,* not *go.* That will be heard later. To be a follower of Jesus, a person must first come.

Come where?

Matthew's Gospel provides an answer packed with meaning. The call of Jesus is *not* an invitation to *do* something; the call is, first of all, to a relationship. Jesus does not say, "Come and do great things." He does not say, "Come and live a virtuous life." He does not say, "Come into the desert and fast for forty days." He says simply…come!

Then, he does something that is key to understanding what it means to become a disciple of Jesus. Although the text is silent on this point, he arranges for Matthew to have dinner with him—at Matthew's house! Did you notice that? It's "Come, Matthew," and the next thing we know he is at table in Matthew's house.

This seems to have been a habit with Jesus. And I daresay it is a habit that continues into our own time. Remember Zacchaeus, also a tax collector like Matthew. Jesus called him down from his tree and then announced, "I must stay at your house today" (Luke 19:5 NRSV). There is great symbolic meaning in the pattern of Jesus calling and then dining with the one called. It tells us that when Jesus says, "Come," it is an invitation to begin an intimate relationship with him in a place where we are most at home—the table where we eat. The place where we share meals is a place of relaxed conversation, a place of sharing, a place of communion. We see in this pattern something that goes on in our lives all the time. If the ear of our heart is properly attuned, if we are listening, we hear this call again and again. *Come.* Come apart and be with me. Be with me in places where you feel most secure, most yourself, most at home.

And is this not what we hear every time we come to the Eucharist? It is more than habit that brings us here, more than a fear of hell or a hope of heaven. When we step through the doors of this church, bless ourselves with holy water, and walk up these aisles, we are hearing that simple word *come.* And we come to this table, which is our common table, the table of the people of St. Joseph's Church. And who joins us there? *Jesus.* Time after time. Habits are hard to break. The habit Jesus revealed in his relationship with Zacchaeus and with Matthew has never changed. Jesus says, "Come," and then he joins us at our table. He joins us for a purpose: to restructure our relationships with God and with others.

But not everyone is capable of hearing that little word *come.* For some the other little word must be spoken. I mean the word *go.* Do you think that the Pharisees standing around the edge of the gathering, whispering about "tax collectors and sinners" were not also invited. Chances are, they were. But they would not come. Why not? Perhaps because their hearts were not ready to hear the word *come.* They had to first hear the word *go.* And so Jesus says, "Go and learn the meaning of the words, 'I desire mercy, not sacrifice.'" (Matt 9:13).

In saying this, Jesus was recalling the prophet Hosea, whom we heard from in the first reading. There, Hosea said, "[F]or it is love that I desire, not sacrifice, and knowledge of God rather than holocausts" (Hos 6:6). The Pharisees were told to go and learn what their ancestors failed to learn from Hosea—God does not reject religious ritual, but ritual loses its meaning when it is uncoupled from knowledge of God.

Hosea struggled long and hard to come to knowledge of God. Hosea uses the expression *daath elohim* to describe Israel's relationship to God,[5] which can be translated as "knowledge of God." One source says that the verb *yada*, from which this expression comes, denotes "an act involving concern, inner engagement, dedication, or attachment to a person."[6] The words *daath elohim* "mean *sympathy for God*, attachment of the whole person, his love as well as his knowledge; an act of involvement, attachment or commitment to God."[7] It means, then, that one who knows God has sympathy, feeling, compassion for God. What is desired is "an inner identification with God rather than a mere dedication to ceremonies."[8]

This is the "knowledge of God" that the Pharisees were sent to learn. And the relationship between God and Israel that Hosea revealed, Jesus proclaimed to be the relationship between God and all humankind. It is a relationship that cannot be observed through ceremonies and rituals alone, although these have their place. Rather, it is a relationship of love, a love that is characterized by intimate attachment, sympathy, compassion, a love whose best analogy is marriage. In sum, before the Pharisees could come to Jesus, they first had to go and learn what God is really like.

We hear the word *come* and sometimes we hear the word *go*. We too must learn *daath elohim*. But once we learn it, we again hear the word *go*. But this time, it is go and be my disciples. Go and preach to the world. Go and baptize in my name. Go in my peace to love and serve the Lord, and one another.

Questions for Further Discussion:

1. Have you heard the words *come* and *go* spoken in your life? In what ways?

2. Have you thought of your relationship with God involving compassion or sympathy for God?

41
YOU ARE THE WIND BENEATH MY WINGS
Eleventh Sunday in Ordinary Time (A)

- Exodus 19:2–6a
- Romans 5:6–11
- Matthew 9:36–10:8

In the Gospel today, Matthew uses the image of sheep to describe the crowds upon whom Jesus looked with pity. He says they were like sheep without a shepherd, "troubled and abandoned" (Matt 9:36). And if you have been around sheep, you would have to agree that the imagery, though unflattering, is quite apt.

I recall a fine summer morning on a trout stream over in Wyoming, watching a shepherd, a young man on horseback, driving a large flock of sheep up a mountain valley. As I watched, a small band of sheep became separated from the flock. For a half-hour, they wandered around in circles, obviously troubled and feeling abandoned, until the shepherd returned and reunited them with the main flock.

Sheep are like that. And if we are honest with ourselves, so are we at times. Blessed Mother Teresa of Calcutta once said that we in the West suffer a poverty greater than the physical poverty she encountered in India. She said that loneliness is the leprosy of Western society. Indeed, that kind of spiritual suffering is a far greater impoverishment than any physical affliction we might suffer.

But the reading from Exodus gives us another image that assures us God is able to lift us out of our troubled and abandoned state. God says to the Hebrew people, and to us, through Moses, "You have seen for yourselves how I treated the Egyptians and how I bore you up on eagle wings, and brought you here to myself" (Exod 19:4). The imagery here is of a mother eagle that encourages her young to take flight and to soar in freedom. The imagery comes from the Hebrew author's observation of how a mother eagle will sometimes support a young eagle on her back until it gains the confidence to let go and fly freely. The Book of Deuteronomy (32:11–12 NRSV) says it even better:

> As an eagle stirs up its nest,
>   and hovers over its young,
> as it spreads its wings, takes them up
>   and bears them aloft on its pinions,
> the LORD alone guided him;
>   no foreign god was with him.

Though we may feel at times like sheep, harassed and helpless, we are destined to be like eagles. God bears us up on eagle wings, supporting us and encouraging us to fly freely.

But we are all young eagles, and, to fly freely, we must let go. Our life is a long process of letting go. From the time we let go of the umbilical cord until the moment we breathe our last breath, we are learning to let go.

We learn to let go of the bad habits we may have been clinging to throughout our adult lives. If we are married, we may have to let go of selfishness toward our spouse: In marriage, we have to let go of bad habits if we are ever to soar in the graced freedom of God's kingdom.

Perhaps we are a young person and must let go of the fear of not being popular because we do not dress or act like someone else. We must let go of all of it, if we are to fly freely like an eagle.

Perhaps we are growing older and clinging to the false security of our own independence; we will have to let go of that too some day and be lifted up by gracious dependence on others.

But we cannot by our own willpower truly let go of whatever we are clinging to. I suspect that the young eagle borne aloft on its mother's wings does not let go and fly freely until it feels the power of the wind beneath its wings.

And so it is with us in our spiritual life. When over time we are able to sense the strong presence of the divine updraft, lifting us up and away, and when we are able to trust that it will always be there, then we can truly let go of whatever is holding us back.

God's love is the wind beneath our wings. God's love enables us to break free of bad habits, free of fears and anxieties that weigh us down, free of all the idolatrous clinging that keeps us from being truly free.

How does God's love become the wind beneath our wings? I believe there is a further hint in the reading from Exodus. God says, "You shall be to me a kingdom of priests, a holy nation" (Exod 19:6). Ours is a mediated religion. One of the ways God's love is mediated to us is through our priests in the sacraments, especially the Eucharist.

But, of course, we are *all*, in a sense, called to be priests, to be mediators of God's love, to be the wind beneath the wings of others. The Second Vatican Council spoke of the priesthood of all believers. We are *not* all called to be ordained priests, but we *are* all called to be priests in the sense that we make possible the flow of God's love into our world. We do that through our patient caring for each other, day after day. And we find as we go along that the more we are able to let go, the more we are able to soar like eagles, the better we are able to bring God's love to those feeling troubled and abandoned.

God asks for more than ordinary goodness from us. God says in Exodus, "You shall be to me a kingdom of priests, a holy nation" (19:6). We are called to be heroic lovers, a holy people. We do not fly away from the world; we simply see it from a different perspective. We are freed from whatever holds us back so that we might help free others. We become the wind of God's love beneath the wings of others.

And when the moment comes for the final thread holding us back to be cut, God will sing to us, "Did I ever tell you, you're my hero? You're everything I hoped you'd be."

And we will sing back to God, "I can fly higher than an eagle, because you are the wind beneath my wings."

Questions for Further Discussion:

1. Have there been times in your life when you felt the wind of God's love beneath your wings? Describe what you felt?

2. How do we become the wind of God's love for others?

42
BROTHER LOVE, BROTHER FEAR
Twelfth Sunday in Ordinary Time (A)

> • Jeremiah 20:10–13
> • Romans 5:12–15
> • Matthew 10:26–33

Three times in today's Gospel Jesus cautions his disciples about fear: "Fear no one.... And do not be afraid of those who kill the body but cannot kill the soul.... So do not be afraid; you are worth more than many sparrows" (Matt 10:26–28). Jesus knew the power of love; he also knew about fear. He knew that fear could paralyze those he loved, thereby keeping them from a deep experience of God's love. The good news of the gospel must transform *both* love *and* fear.

The fourteenth-century mystic, Julian of Norwich, was gifted with a keen insight into these twin forces. She says this in her *Showings:*

> Love and fear are brothers, and they are rooted in us by the good-ness of our Creator, and they will never be taken from us without end. It is our nature to love, and we are given grace to love; and it is our nature to fear, and we are given grace to fear. It is proper to God's lordship and his fatherhood to be feared, as it is proper to his goodness to be loved; and it is proper to us who are his ser-vants and his children to fear him, for his lordship and father-hood, as it is proper to us to love him for his goodness. And yet this reverent fear and love are not the same, but they are different in kind and in effect, and neither of them may be obtained with-out the other.[9]

Brother Love. Brother Fear. These are our companions on the journey
to God, for they are a part of our God-given nature, which we must
acknowledge and integrate. They are not the same but, through the
grace of Christ, both can be transformed into friends and helpers on
the way. Each must undergo a conversion if we are to realize the joy of
God that is our heritage.

 Brother Fear. Brother Fear is that part of us which is preoccupied
with what *might* happen. Brother Fear reminds us of death, reminds us
of our own limitations, our fragilities. We know this part of ourselves
every time we find ourselves in crisis: the dilemma of disaster and
opportunity. Then, the good brother works on our memory:
"Remember your limitations. Remember how you failed before.
Remember the time you panicked, the time in the fourth grade when
you stood before the class and did not know the answer." Remember.
Remember. Remember. Brother Fear works in our memory. And the
effect is a cold dread of what *might* happen.

Brother Fear is converted by the words of Jesus: "Be not afraid.
Do not fear events that might even kill your body. They cannot touch
that part of you known only to me." The words of Jesus that come to
us from our memory melt the icy grip of fear and free our natural talent and ability. Certainly, Brother Fear has a place in our lives. We
need to know our limitations, what is possible. But Brother Fear cannot dominate our lives to the point where we are rendered ineffective.

The transformation that must take place in Brother Fear is mir-
rored in the conversion experience of Brother Love. We are on similar ground in dealing with this brother. Brother Love will try to
convince us that we were made to find our happiness in something less
than God. Using such good things as pleasure, material wealth and
power, security, prestige, this good brother will seek to keep us fixed
on the tentative as our final end, rather than as a means to an end. The
diversion from our true purpose in life that comes about through an
unredeemed Brother Love can be just as real as that produced by
Brother Fear. Both can leave us frozen in our development, impeded
in our growth into God.

Each of these companions on the journey, Brother Fear and
Brother Love, has a true purpose, a true role to play. Brother Fear
must be converted from an attitude of worried anticipation of what
might happen into an attitude of reverent fear of God. By fear of God
is not meant a fear of retribution. It is not a fear of God's wrath that
must become the dominant pattern of our life but rather an abiding
awe before a provident, all-merciful God. When Brother Fear habitu-

ally turns us to God in a humble, reverent stance, then the necessary conversion is taking place.

In the same way, when Brother Love has moved beyond a selfish grasping of limited good things and begins to see all of creation as gift, helping us on the way, then real transformation is underway.

In the end, these two brothers—Brother Love, Brother Fear—must be reconciled. They cannot live separated like the brothers Cain and Abel whose rivalry over God's blessing ended in violence and death (Genesis 4). Rather, they must grow and mature like the brothers Jacob and Esau who, despite their differences, reconciled after a long separation. Let us pray in this Mass for that reconciliation in our lives.

Questions for Further Discussion:

1. Do you agree with Julian of Norwich that love and fear are brothers? Are you aware of their presence in your life? How?

2. How do we reconcile the two?

43
RADICAL SIMPLICITY
Thirteenth Sunday in Ordinary Time (A)

- 2 Kings 4:8–11, 14–16a
- Romans 6:3–4, 8–11
- Matthew 10:37–42

At the heart of holiness is radical simplicity, not easily achieved, but essential for those who desire to love Jesus.

Every religious tradition has, I am sure, stories that express the truth found in today's Gospel: To reach perfection, enlightenment, purity of heart—whatever you want to call it—there must be an uncompromising commitment to let go of all things. I find this truth expressed in stories from the desert fathers, the Hasidic Jewish tradition, the Zen Buddhist tradition, as well as the Gospel. Let me give you one example:

Ryokan, a Zen master, lived the simplest kind of life in a little hut at the foot of a mountain. One evening a thief visited the hut only to discover there nothing in it to steal.

Ryokan returned and caught him. "You may have come a long way to visit me," he told the prowler, "and you should not return empty-handed. Please take my clothes as a gift."

The thief was bewildered. He took the clothes and slunk away.

Ryokan sat naked, watching the moon. "Poor fellow," he mused, "I wish I could give him this beautiful moon."[10]

Although he was not a Christian, Ryokan knew what Jesus knew: Radical simplicity is the key to freedom. Although he never used the words, Jesus was teaching radical simplicity, for it was only by such a change of life that his disciples could become the kind of missionaries the world of their time needed. Radical simplicity: needed then, desperately needed now.

Jesus did not demand this approach simply to impose an extreme ascetic on his followers, nor did he intend that families be abandoned or looked down upon. Indeed, he says later in chapter 15: "Honor your father and your mother." No, Jesus had something life-giving in mind. He was leading those he loved to the kind of deep transformation necessary for gospel living. That transformation is always contingent upon our willingness to open up more space in our hearts for God. Or, the great Dominican, Meister Eckhart, might go even further and say that as long as we are simply creating space for God, we have yet to fully experience the inbreaking of God. It is when there is no more separate space, when God, in a sense, becomes our heart, that we know and love Jesus in the way today's Gospel is suggesting.

This is a radical way of explaining the Gospel, but then the good news was always intended to be radical—but radical for a reason. It is radical in its demands so that the freedom, which is its result, might be just as radical. That is the effect of a commitment to love Jesus more than anything else—freedom. As long as we are attached to self and our self-satisfying ways of living, we will never know the tremendous freedom that comes with embracing that most exquisite of paradoxes Jesus left us: "Whoever finds his life will lose it, and whoever loses his life for my sake will find it" (Matt 10:39).

Ironically, the life of radical simplicity, and the freedom that is its fruit, enabled Ryokan, and others like him from all religious traditions, to manifest the other great sign of religious transformation—hospitality. The unnamed woman in the first reading who hosted Elisha must have had the same attitude toward guests as did Ryokan, the Zen master. She freely gave the prophet what she had, much the way the unnamed widow had fed the prophet Elijah with her few remaining scraps of food when he was in need. (1 Kgs 17). For their hospitality, each received the gift of life. Perhaps these stories were in the mind of Jesus when he reminded us that a cup of cold water given to a little one will win a reward.

We probably miss the reward that comes with hospitality time and time again because we have not recognized the value of radical simplicity. It seems clear to me that the more possessions someone has the less generous that person is in hospitality to little ones. My own experience in rural Mexico taught me that. It was the peasants, as poor as Zen Master Ryokan, who were the most generous. And have they received a prophet's reward? Perhaps. Their hospitality helped form me and has kept them in my heart and mind ever since. When I sift through the stacks of charitable solicitations that come to my door every day, I always look for their faces and see them as representatives of the third-world poor.

I heard recently that if everyone in the world consumed natural resources the way we do in North America, we would need four additional planets just to meet those needs. We live in great affluence in this part of the world. And we live in fear that what we have may be taken away from us. How far our attitude toward life is from that of Ryokan! How far from the words of Jesus in the Gospel.

Simplify! Simplify! So said Thoreau. It is the way to freedom, the way to the fullness of life Jesus promised.

Questions for Further Discussion:

1. Do you see living a simple life as part of the way of Jesus?
2. How do you need to simplify your life?

44
REVEALING GOD TO OUR WORLD
Fourteenth Sunday in Ordinary Time (A)

- Zechariah 9:9–10
- Romans 8:9, 11–13
- Matthew 11:25–30

If my complexion seems a bit ruddier this morning, it's because I just got back from a five-day backpacking trip through the Wind Rivers in

Wyoming, one of the most beautiful places on earth. A few days ago I was hiking at ten-thousand feet through alpine meadows with the fragrance of lupine floating on mountain breezes cooled by melting snowfields. Close by, where the snow banks had receded, tiny buttercups, crocuses, and bluebells had poked through the thin soil, blossoming gloriously during their brief window of summer. Ice-cold water trickled and cascaded down the rough granite slopes, pine trees stirred in the gentle breezes; our packs were light, the trail was easy.

As we hiked along I thought about the ancient Celts and their notion of "thin places." The Celts believed there were "thin places" in this world, usually in some idyllic natural setting where the dividing line between this life and life in the heavenly kingdom was very thin. At these places, it seemed one could almost cross over to the next life.

So, as I walked along, I said to our Lord, "Lord, this is about as close to heaven as I am going to get. Can't I just cross over?" And then I remembered I had promised our pastor, Father Colin, I would be back to preach this weekend, so I said, "I guess we will have to hold off on that for now."

But my recent commune with nature is relevant to the Gospel we heard today, for it is about the revealing of God. One of the ways God is revealed is in the Book of Nature. It is in the presence of nature, of wildness, that we experience awe and wonder, which are the start of religious experience. The psalmist knew this when he wrote:

> When I look at your heavens, the work of your fingers,
>   the moon and the stars that you have established;
> what are human beings that you are mindful of them,
>   mortals that you care for them?
>
> Yet you have made them a little lower than God,
>   and crowned them with glory and honor. (Ps 8:3–5 NRSV)

And yet we know that the Source of all creation, the God who created majestic mountains and tiny alpine flowers, *does* care for humankind. But it is more than care. Nature is the loving, creative activity of a Divine Artist who has crafted a world of extravagant beauty to attract us to the Creator. Someone said that creation has been made so beautiful that in contemplating that beauty we might come to recognize the Creator. In nature God is like a lover who makes herself beautiful down to the tiniest detail so that her beloved might be attracted and fall in love with her. *We* are that beloved. And what joy it must bring to the heart of God when someone, attracted by that great beauty, discovers the beauty of God, and falls in love with the Creator! When that happens, we can say with St. John of the Cross: "Mine are the heavens and mine is the earth. Mine are the nations, the just are mine, and mine the sinners. The angels are mine, and the mother of God, and all things are mine; and God himself is mine and for me, because Christ is mine and all for me."[11]

But God did not stop with the Book of Nature. God gave us as well the Book of Scripture, the Book of God's Word. In this book, God is also revealed as a God who creates and sustains. But there is more of God revealed in this book. From the opening lines of Genesis to the final words of Revelation, God is revealed as a God who enters into human history, a God who longs to be in loving relationship with all of humankind, starting with the people of Israel.

God is revealed as a jealous God, a God who will go to any lengths to preserve a covenant of love, a God who will follow his unfaithful beloved wherever she may wander, with the hope of bringing her back.

God is revealed as a God who makes promises—and keeps them. One of those promises God makes is to send a savior, a redeemer, someone who will restore once and for all that loving relationship God intended from the beginning. We believe that promise was fulfilled in Jesus of Nazareth.

Jesus says in the Gospel today, "[N]o one knows the Father except the Son and anyone to whom the Son wishes to reveal him" (Matt 11:27). Jesus is the ultimate revelation of God. Through Jesus, God is revealed in ways we cannot find in the Book of Nature or in the Book of Scripture. In Jesus we encounter God directly, not through the veil of nature or symbols. We encounter God as Love revealed through Jesus Christ. For us as Catholics, that revelation reaches its highest level in the Liturgy of the Eucharist. There, all our senses cooperate to reveal a God present in the beauty of music, in postures of unity, in harmony and peace, in sign and symbol. God is revealed as a God who becomes food for us, divine food, food that nourishes not just our bodies but our minds and hearts and spirits. God is revealed as a God who not only comes among us but who becomes an intimate part of us.

And when we leave here this morning, we need be reminded of one further important truth. God is revealed through us. God does not stay hidden in us. For better or for worse, we reveal God to those around us. But we cannot reveal what we have yet to experience. If we have not experienced God in the wonder of nature, then we will likely remain silent when we see the rivers made ugly by pollution, or the air fouled with smog, or the land torn up and wasted. If we haven't encountered the God of loving, faithful relationships revealed in scripture, we will be less able to enter into such relationships with our family, friends, those with whom we work. And if God has not been revealed to us through Jesus Christ, then a hungry world will be further frustrated when it looks to us for nourishment.

We live in a world that rarely recognizes God in nature, seldom seeks God in the written word, and has, in large part, yet to experience God as food and drink. We are the ones who must reveal God to the world. We are the ones who must find God revealed in thousands of places. We must be the mediators of God to our world.

Questions for Further Discussion:

1. Do you experience God as revealed in the Book of Nature? Book of Scripture? Jesus Christ?
2. How do you reveal God to other people?

45
JESUS THE GOOD FARMER
Fifteenth Sunday in Ordinary Time (A)

- Isaiah 55:10–11
- Romans 8:18–23
- Matthew 13:1–23

Jesus was one of the greatest teachers of all times. But as any teacher knows, there is nothing more frustrating than trying to teach students who do not fully comprehend what you are saying. At the start of today's Gospel, you can almost hear Jesus saying to himself, "They don't get it. They just don't get it." Thus, he quotes Isaiah, "You shall indeed hear but not understand, you shall indeed look but never see" (Matt 13:14).

And, of course, these words are meant for us and our world as well. Despite twenty centuries of preaching the gospel, we live in a world that *still* does not get it.

Jesus had an excellent understanding of human nature. He knew the human condition. He knew that a frontal assault on disbelief would not work. And so he uses the teaching device of telling a story. He knows that people love a good story, especially one that has a hook in it to hold the attention and to keep the mind pondering its real meaning.

Jesus tells a story that helps us understand why the joy and peace of the gospel message is not always present in our lives. He uses images that could be readily grasped by his listeners, and by us. He tells a story about several different types of soil.

If we reflect on our lives in the light of this story, we may be able to gain a better understanding of our own lack of faith at times. Ultimately, it is a story full of hope, for Jesus promises that the good soil will yield a harvest of as much as a hundredfold.

We believe that God created us as good, rich soil. But at some point we may become aware that the soil has hardened. It may be the coarseness, the crudeness of our popular culture that treads upon our souls, day after day, week after week, eventually creating a hard path where the good seed scattered by Jesus, the Good Farmer, cannot penetrate and take root.

Or perhaps the seeds of a faith-filled life have taken root but they have been choked out by a preoccupation with success in the world, with worry and fears, with bad habits.

If we have ears to hear, we can reflect on this Gospel and recognize what has produced the hard, rocky, thorn-filled soil in our lives where the divine seeds cannot flourish.

Jesus was an excellent teacher. But Jesus must have known that even the best parables could not break up the hard ground of every human heart. It would take more than penetrating words. It would require his own suffering, death, and resurrection to accomplish the task of creating soil where the gospel might flourish. And that is where the hope lies. The work of preparing good soil in our lives, and in all the world, has been done by Jesus. And that work goes on.

Christ is constantly at work in our lives, breaking up the hard ground of our hearts, encouraging us to root out the thorns that choke out real growth and preparing us for an abundant harvest. Sometimes suffering comes upon us unexpectedly, painfully, and can seem meaningless, even absurd. But if we see that suffering in the light of faith, we are able to recognize it as the work of Christ, the Good Farmer, preparing the soil of our hearts for greater growth.

But, of course, this work requires our cooperation. There is another story about a farmer that, I think, Jesus would have liked.

A farmer had worked hard at his farm for many years. He had plowed the fields, cleared away weeds and brush, constructed sturdy and attractive barns and granaries. One day, he was visited by the pastor from his church. They toured the farm, and the minister repeatedly commented, "Look what you and God have done with this farm.

See how you and God have turned this farm into a beautiful and productive place." Finally, the farmer turned to the minister and said, "Yes, Reverend, but you should have seen it when God was working it by himself."

It is hard work to cooperate with God in transforming hard, rocky soil into good, rich soil. It is hard work to come to Mass every Sunday; it is hard work to read the scriptures consistently and to be faithful in our prayers and devotions.

But there is a wonderful promise in the Gospel that keeps us faithful to that work. It is the promise of our Lord that our faithful efforts will be rewarded thirty, sixty, even a hundred times over. That is not hyperbole, that is a promise.

We must never lose sight of the fact that we are made of *good* soil. If at times that soil seems hard, or rocky, or choked with thorns, remember that the parable ends by talking about the good, rich, fertile soil that is present in all of us. That is the soil that gives us hope. By our being here we testify that our soil, whatever it may be, is open to the word of God which, as Isaiah says, falls from the heavens like rain and snow and does not return until it has watered the earth, making it fertile and fruitful.

We open ourselves now to receive that gift, confident that the divine seeds planted in our rich soil will grow and yield a hundredfold.

Questions for Further Discussion:

1. How would you describe the soil that is you? Has it changed over time? What made it change?

2. What can be done to make our soil more productive?

46
MY SINS ARE RUNNING OUT BEHIND ME
Sixteenth Sunday in Ordinary Time (A)

- Wisdom 12:13, 16–19
- Romans 8:26–27
- Matthew 13:24–43

Jesus scattered stories on the earth the way a farmer scatters seed. Some fell on deaf ears and never took root. They were simply forgotten. But some, like the three parables in today's Gospel, fell on attentive ears, took root, and flourished, leaving behind seeds that would sprout and bear fruit over time.

Here is a story that is a descendant of the first of today's parables—the parable of the weeds growing with the wheat. It comes from that great collection of wisdom left to us by a group of desert dwellers whom we call the desert fathers, those zealous Christians who left the cities in order to live holy lives in the wastelands of Egypt and Palestine. (There were desert mothers too who have also left us some equally delightful stories[12]). I think Jesus would have liked this story as much as the ones he told.

> A brother in Scete happened to commit a fault, and the elders assembled, and sent for Abbot Moses to join them. He, however, did not want to come. The priest sent him a message, saying: Come, the community of the brethren is waiting for you. So he arose and started off. And taking with him a very old basket full of holes, he filled it with sand, and carried it behind him. The elders came out to meet him, and said: What is this, Father? The elder replied: My sins are running out behind me, and I do not see them, and today I come to judge the sins of another! They, hearing this, said nothing to the brother but pardoned him.[13]

Abbot Moses knew what the kingdom of heaven is all about. It's about *not* judging others! That is what Jesus is telling us in the parable of the weeds growing amidst the wheat.

In this first parable, also called the parable of the wheat and the tares, Jesus used story to teach what he had previously declared explicitly: "Do not judge, so that you may not be judged" (Matt 7:1 NRSV). He said this, knowing that judging deprives us of the joy of the kingdom. We cannot know true kingdom joy unless we learn about this special kingdom.

This kingdom is not like a nation state, or a political entity, that you become a part of through birth or naturalization. Rather, the kingdom of heaven is something we experience in the depths of our being, when our ways conform to the ways of God. It is a kingdom discovered not through traveling over great distances, but by entering into the depths of our own being through prayer and meditation.

We cannot enter the kingdom Jesus is speaking of if we are preoccupied with judging—both others and our own selves. Judging is a divisive activity that blocks the kingdom from coming into being within us. When we think, or say, "I like that person but *not* that one," we are engaging in behavior that divides and, because it divides, takes away true joy. We may even have good reasons for preferring one person over another, but the act of comparing, of judging and assigning relative value to what we regard as good or bad is inherently destructive. Our judging becomes like the actions of a foolish farmer who, in an attempt to pull out the weeds, destroys the wheat as well, its roots being inextricably intertwined with the roots of its neighbor.

The roots of the weeds and wheat are intertwined, because in planting them, God did not make distinctions the way we do. God is one; God is not divided. God expresses no preference over weeds and wheat. Matthew says, "[H]e makes his sun rise on the evil and on the good, and sends rain on the righteous and on the unrighteous" (Matt 5:45 NRSV). If God does not judge, how can *we* justify our own judging? To be holy we must be like God. And when we act in ways that are contrary to God's ways, the kingdom does not come; it disappears.

Jesus knew that, if we continued in the very human habit of judging others, we would never experience the kingdom as a way of being, as an experience of holiness that grows secretly and slowly like a mustard plant. Jesus knew that our judging neutralizes the kingdom yeast growing within us. Jesus knew that, to live as kingdom people, we must first die to the ego-driven sin of judging.

Having said that, I must hasten to add this bit of paradox: We must not *judge*, but we must still make *judgments*. Every day we are required to make judgments, whether it is a choice of vegetables, a choice of friends, or a choice between two job applicants. A judge in a courtroom must make judgments all the time but may still be firmly grounded in the kingdom of heaven. Why? Because such judgments arise out of a duty to serve justice, not out of a divided heart. When such judgments are demanded, we simply make them and go on. But if our necessary judgments cause separation from another person, the best we can do is to always keep that person in our heart, praying and willing the best for him or her.

It takes disciplined effort to reduce and gradually overcome the destructive judging, the kingdom-excluding judging, that is a part of our human condition. But as we persist in prayer and meditation, we not only become more aware of our judging propensity, we begin to develop a taste for living more and more a life of "choiceless awareness." We acknowledge the things we do not like as well as those things that attract us. While we may choose one or the other, we do so with a graced equanimity. When we are able to accept all things, then we can make our own the words of Job, "[T]he LORD gave, and the Lord has taken away; blessed be the name of the LORD" (Job 1:21 NRSV).

Questions for Further Discussion:

1. Is it possible to live without judging others?
2. What is meant by "choiceless awareness"?

47
WHOM DO WE TRUST?
Seventeenth Sunday in Ordinary Time (A)

- 1 Kings 3:5, 7–12
- Romans 8:28–30
- Matthew 13:44–52

There is probably no harder statement to accept than the one we heard in the second reading. Paul says to the Romans, "We know that all things work for good for those who love God, who are called according to his purpose" (Rom 8:28).

How can we believe this to be true, when our own experience seems to tell us otherwise? How can we believe that all things work for good when a baby dies? Or when a young man in his prime, beloved by his family and by his country, dies suddenly in a tragic airplane crash? How can we believe this when tragedy or disaster strikes us in our personal lives?

There are no easy answers to these questions. *None.* And we do not do justice to them by giving simplistic or naïve answers. When we struggle with Paul's statement, we are confronting profound mystery.

But there is a key to approaching mystery. The key is to ask: Whom do we trust? Do we trust the voices of our secular society, which tell us that belief in a God who ultimately brings good out of evil is absurd? Or do we listen to and trust the voices of our own tradition where we meet those who, through faith, came to embrace the truth that all things work for good for those who love God?

Do we trust the voice of Solomon in the first reading? Solomon, the man to whom God gave a heart so wise and understanding that we still speak of the "wisdom of Solomon." Why was Solomon given such a heart? Because he asked for it. The Lord says to Solomon, "Because you have asked for this—not for a long life for yourself, nor for riches, nor for the life of your enemies, but for understanding so that you may know what is right—I do as you requested" (1 Kgs 3:10–12). Do we trust Solomon enough to believe that we too can pray for and receive an understanding heart?

Do we trust St. Paul, the great evangelist whose experience of the risen Christ was so powerful it knocked him to the ground on the way to Damascus?

Do we trust the great mystic, Julian of Norwich, who in the fourteenth century was given a series of visions, whose content she expressed in these words, "But all will be well, and all will be well and every manner of thing will be well"?[14]

Do we trust our Lord Jesus, who in the moment of his greatest agony prayed, "Father, if you are willing, remove this cup from me; yet not my will but yours be done" (Luke 22:42 NRSV)?

Do we trust the voices of others in our own parish community here at St. Joseph enough to come together and reflect on God's word? Renew 2000 gave us the opportunity to do just that.

I suspect we do not trust the voices of our own tradition, because we do not hear them; we let the noise of our world drown them out. The voices of our tradition are unobtrusive. They do not intrude like the constant stream of information and commercial propaganda that comes at us from all sides through the media. The voices of Solomon, of Paul, Julian and our Lord do not come to us dressed up like the voices of our culture. The voices of our tradition do not captivate our sensual imagination, as do the voices of our popular culture; we have to make an effort to hear them and to trust them.

It takes time to develop trust. We do not trust another person unless we have spent considerable time with that person. The same is true with the voices from our tradition. If we do not know who Solomon was, if we have not sat with Paul or Julian and pondered their words, if we have not meditated on the life of Christ, if we have not shared our faith with others, we cannot expect to trust their voices.

But this is an area where a little bit goes a long way. A small amount of time spent every day with scripture, with reading the lives of the saints gradually over time, produces a marvelous result. A knowledge of God's ways begins to grow and replace the fear and the doubts that are so often present in our lives.

And then there comes a time when we have that experience Jesus was talking about in the Gospel—the experience of finding a treasure so valuable, a pearl of such great price that we are willing to give up everything to possess it. This treasure is the knowledge of God, the mystery of faith that is unlocked by the key of trust.

We do not find that rich prize easily. But in looking for treasure, it helps to know where to look. Sometimes the events of our own lives are the secret hiding place for that treasure. We will find our treasure by listening to the voices of those in our tradition whom we trust. And when we find it, we are able to say with Paul that, indeed, all things work for good for those who love God.

Whom do we trust? What answer do you give?

Questions for Further Discussion:

1. Whom in our tradition do you trust? Why?
2. Do you believe that all things work together for good?

48

THE GOLDEN THREAD OF COMPASSION
Eighteenth Sunday in Ordinary Time (A)

- Isaiah 55:1–3
- Romans 8:35, 37–38
- Matthew 14:13–21

There are some lines from the poet William Blake that come to mind when I reflect on today's Gospel:

> I give you the end of a golden string,
> Only wind it into a ball,
> It will lead you in at Heaven's Gate
> Built in Jerusalem's wall.

Blake's imagery can evoke many different interpretations. But we might say in the context of today's Gospel reading that the golden string is *compassion*. Woven through *all* of the Gospel is the compassion of Our Lord. Another name we might use for Christ is the "Divine Compassion."

Compassion is defined as "a feeling of deep sympathy and sorrow for another who is stricken by suffering or misfortune accompanied by a strong desire to alleviate the pain or remove its cause" (*Random*

House Dictionary). *Compassion* comes from the Latin roots *cum*, meaning "with," and *passio*, "to suffer"; hence, to suffer with someone. God had such compassion for the world, that God came into the world in order to suffer with us and help us learn about compassion. Christ is the embodiment of God suffering with humankind.

In the Gospel today we see how compassion is the golden thread that leads to heaven's gate. Jesus is alone, in a boat, in a deserted place, grieving the death of John the Baptist. But as he mourns for his kinsman, compassion moves him to resume his ministry of healing and of nourishing those who followed him. The text says, "[H]is heart was moved with pity for them" (Matt 14:14). Compassion was the golden thread that led Jesus back to caring for people.

We might learn from this example when we are grieving, not so much for the loss of a loved one, but when we find ourselves grieving for ourselves. When we find ourselves grieving the many losses we suffer in a lifetime—the loss of youth, lost opportunities, loss of health, and the inevitable loss of our life—compassion for others can restore us to life. When we grieve the many injuries of life, some real, some imagined, some inflicted by others, some self-inflicted, compassion is the golden thread that leads us back to the healthy way of life God intended for us, a life of caring for others. The force of compassion that moved Jesus is the same force at work in us. The golden thread of compassion leads us to heaven's gate.

And when Divine Compassion encounters human trust, a miracle occurs. We see that later in this Gospel scene as Jesus, still following the golden thread of compassion, feels the suffering of people who are hungry and tired. But notice that the miracle did not result just from the compassion of Jesus. Someone in the crowd had food and, more importantly, was willing to share it with others. Someone had five loaves of bread and two fish, and was generous with them.

It takes trust to be generous, to share hospitality with others. It takes trust to know that even when you have but a little, you can share it with others. Trust is the confident knowledge that no matter how little we have, there will be enough to go around. The person who shared his or her food trusted that there would be enough to go around. And there was. When Divine Compassion finds human trust, miracles happen. In this case, the "feeding of the five thousand" or "the multiplication of the loaves and fishes."

Many of us have encountered such human trust. After my first year of college, I spent the summer in southern Oaxaca, Mexico, working with a Maryknoll priest. There, I came to know poor people who had very little to share. They lived without electricity, without paved roads, without running water, in dirt-floor houses. What food they had came directly from the land, not from a grocery store.

My wife and I went back to visit these villagers five years later, and, as we got ready to leave, they came forward with gifts of what little they had. The aging Señora Sosa gave us one egg, perhaps representing what one chicken might produce in several weeks. Others brought fruit. And the lean, sad-faced Señor Peralta gave us a chunk of dried venison, one of the few sources of protein in that primitive area. Their generosity arose from a deep trust that, despite great scarcity, there would be enough to go around.

Was there a miracle that day in that tiny Mexican village? In a way, yes, for the example of their generosity formed me in an important way. It was for me a graced experience. Divine Compassion encounters human trust and a miracle takes place every time.

Divine Compassion continues to be at work in our world. God continues to suffer with each one of us. Jesus has revealed God as Compassion. Our God is not like the gods of the Greeks who manipulated humans, finding amusement in the ebb and flow of human suffering. Our God has followed the golden thread of compassion right into our world and will never leave it.

In a few minutes we will experience again the miracle of today's Gospel when we celebrate the Eucharist together. When the gifts are brought forward, we reenact the trust of that unknown follower of Jesus who brought forward gifts of bread and fish. But we bring forward more than material gifts. We bring as well the gifts of all our suffering, all our hurting, all the pain we encounter every day, all the loss we experience in life, all the injuries. We bring it all to the altar, trusting that Christ welcomes our gifts, longs to receive our suffering, and accepts each tiny bit of it. Human trust again meets Divine Compassion and a miracle occurs.

What happens in the Eucharist will always be hidden in mystery. But we can say this: Nourished by the body and blood of Christ, we leave this assembly, we go out into our community as other Christs to follow the golden thread of compassion, wherever it may lead. We become the means by which the Divine Compassion touches our suffering world. Follow the golden thread when you leave here today. It will lead you in "at Heaven's Gate, Built in Jerusalem's wall."

Questions for Further Discussion:

1. Where is the golden thread of compassion leading you?
2. Where have you experienced compassion in your life?

49

TO CARE AND NOT TO CARE
Nineteenth Sunday in Ordinary Time (A)

- 1 Kings 19:9a, 11–13a
- Romans 9:1–5
- Matthew 14:22–33

In his poem, "Ash Wednesday," T. S. Eliot gives us some words that shed light on today's Gospel:

> Blessed sister, holy mother, spirit of the fountain,
>   spirit of the garden,
> Suffer us not to mock ourselves with falsehood
> Teach us to care and not to care
> Teach us to sit still
> Even among these rocks,
> Our peace in His will....[15]

"Teach us to care and not to care." That is the lesson from this Gospel: learning to care and not to care. When we care, we travel light; when "care" turns to "cares," we sink like a stone.

A dramatic scene is set for us: a small band of disciples on troubled waters, weary bodies struggling against a powerful storm, a tiny craft tossed from wave to wave. Think: perfect storm!

Now, these were men who knew the hard reality of storms. These were men who were no strangers to wind, rain, and crashing waves. But the terror of the sea was only part of their nightmare. It is the ghost that gets to them. A figure moves toward them, a ghostly figure, picking its way between the swells and troughs of this perfect storm. Matthew says simply, "They were terrified."

Hard to believe, but Jesus was the cause of their terror. Not the Jesus they had known but a Jesus, perfectly calm in the midst of chaos, walking on the water!

You would think that Peter would simply invite Jesus into the boat. But Peter was the impulsive one. He had to go to Jesus. He says, "Lord, if it is you, command me to come to you on the water" (Matt 14:28).

And Jesus obliges. "Come," he says! "Come, Peter, you who are to be head of my Church! Come! Come across the troubled waters! Come into the chaos of the storm! Take the risk of wind and wave! Come to the source of your peace and salvation!"

"Teach us to care and not to care."

For a while Peter does just fine. He travels light. He is moved only by care, that state of thinking about the other to the exclusion of self, that willingness to leave the ego-centered safety of one's known world and plunge into the unknown.

Peter cares for Jesus. Care impels him to be with Jesus, despite great risk. And perhaps it is also care for his fellow sailors crouching in their small craft that compels him to step out in faith. Peter travels light, without the heavy weight of fear, without cares; his care is for the Other, Jesus, his Lord and Master. And his care is for a Church in embryo, huddled precariously in the bottom of his boat.

Care is the foundation of love. The poet Joy Harjo says in her poem, "Day of the Dead," "Love changes molecular structure."[16] That is what happened that night on the Sea of Galilee. That explains Peter's first steps. Peter was moved by love built on the foundation of care. His love changed the molecular structure of his path, and he moved lightly along it.

But there is a paradox here—"teach us to care and not to care." *Care* lives in tension with *cares*.

Suddenly something happens. The molecular structure shifts. A tiny, little letter is Peter's doom—the letter *s*. *Care* becomes *cares*. The molecular structure of cares is fear. Fear drives out faith.

Fear now grabs at Peter's ankles. Doubt entraps his steps. The gravity of the situation overpowers him. The wind drives away his care for Jesus and his companions. And in its place come cares, cares about his own safety, sweeping over him, clouding his vision. He no longer sees Jesus. Peter is true to his name—he sinks like a *Rock*!

Then comes the prayer that should be constantly on our lips, "Lord, save me!" It is a prayer that captures our deepest longing. "Lord, save me." When care is replaced by cares, and we find ourselves sinking, our prayer can only be, "Lord, save me."

Peter must have reflected on this experience throughout the remainder of his life, for he left us a key piece of wisdom. Peter was later to tell his little Church, "Cast all your anxiety [cares] on him, because he cares for you" (1 Pet 5:7 NRSV). After a lifetime of reflection, Peter must have realized he was unsinkable that night, had he known then what he knew later: "Cast all your cares on him." Had he done so, this Gospel scene would have ended much differently.

We are Peter in our daily lives. Every day, we hear the words of Jesus, "Come!" We step out of the boat. We move toward Jesus, who appears in so many forms. But then something distracts us. Cares begin to weigh us down. Our feet become leaden. Fear grips us. We begin to sink. That is when Peter is there to remind us—"Cast your cares on him." We cannot make the journey through the chaos of life if we are burdened with cares.

Walking on water can be a tricky business, a risky adventure, a journey fraught with danger. But we are called to do just that. Those who go that way must travel light. Those who hope to make it must cast their cares on the Lord.

Now is the time to cobble up all your cares and toss them to Jesus as he stands amid the chaos, saying, "Come."

Those are easy words to speak. But oh how difficult to apply in practice. Our daily lives are plagued by cares, by fears that dissipate faith and leave us sinking.

How do we live without care?

Keep in mind that Jesus comes to us in a thousand different ways, always eager to take our cares upon himself. We have only to give them up.

He comes to us in the sacrament of reconciliation. Leave your cares with him there.

He comes to us in this very assembly, in the proclaiming of the word, in the Eucharist.

Toss your cares to him as the collection basket goes by.

He comes to us in our prayer. Take his consolation; leave him your cares.

He comes to us in the form of a dear friend who is willing to listen. Pass your cares to Jesus via letters, telephone calls, e-mail. He will accept them. No questions asked.

He comes to us when we express our cares in a journal, give them form in poetry, or articulate them in an essay.

Jesus comes to you in nature to take your cares. Recall T. S. Eliot's words—Leave your cares with your blessed sister, your holy mother, the spirit of the fountain, the spirit of the garden; they will get to Jesus.

Sit still, even among the rocks. And leave your cares there.

Give your cares to Jesus, and you will walk lightly through life. You will not sink. Learn the lesson, "To care and not to care."

Questions for Further Discussion:

1. Are you able to care and not to care?
2. Where in your life does Jesus come to take away your cares?

50
THE PASSION OF MARY
Assumption Vigil (A)

- 1 Chronicles 15:3–4, 15–16; 16:1–2
- 1 Corinthians 15:54b–57
- Luke 11:27–28

Reactions I heard to Mel Gibson's movie, *The Passion of the Christ*, have been mixed. Some have loved it; others like myself found it excessively violent. But one consistent comment I heard is how appealing the images of Mary are in the movie. Many of those who felt numbed by the disproportionate depiction of Jesus' suffering found a kind of relief in identifying with Mary in her own passion. One of the most touching of such reactions came from a close family member who, a few years ago, lost a son to Lou Gehrigs disease (ALS).

My nephew, Andy, was the kind of young man who would have been at home among Jesus' little band of followers. Strong, yet gentle— some referred to him as "The Gentle Giant"—he was the kind of young man who could have fished all night with James and John, or worked all day using Jesus' carpenter tools to build a house. So robust was Andy that none of us believed it when he came back from the doctor with the diagnosis of an incurable disease. But over the course of the next two years, we witnessed the slow wasting away of a once strong, healthy young man, until at last, the mysterious disease ended Andy's life at age thirty-eight.

When she watched *The Passion of the Christ*, Andy's mother identified easily and naturally with Mary. She had been there. She had known the agony, the helplessness, and the brokenheartedness Mary felt. She could walk with Mary, weep with her, and, in the end, sympathize with her in the inevitability of death. Mary was a source of comfort because she walked the same excruciating path so many mothers have had to travel.

The experience many had of Mary's passion within *The Passion* helps us to understand why we honor Mary with the feast of the Assumption. The proper place for Mary in the Church and in the world has never been on a pedestal; it has always been among those who suffer. The words of Jesus in tonight's Gospel point to that truth. Mary did not claim for herself an exalted place in the hierarchy of saints. She was blessed, not only for carrying the Source of all blessing in her womb, but, as Jesus says, for hearing the word of God and obeying it. The word took flesh in Mary's womb, but it also found a home in her heart, a heart that would thereafter beat with compassion for those who endure suffering and loss.

Hearing the word of God and obeying it was no more a simple task for Mary than it is for us. Though we speak of Mary as a woman of faith, she was not spared the difficulty every parent experiences in seeking to understand a child. She too knew confusion, anxiety, and doubt, starting with the first angelic announcement that she, as yet unmarried, would bear a son named Jesus who would be called Son of God. (Luke 1:26–38). Mary was "amazed" at what Simeon said of her son but she must have also pondered throughout her life the old prophet's words to her, "[A] sword will pierce your own soul too." (Luke 2:35 NRSV). The words are a reminder that because she loved her son, Mary would undergo her own passion.

The struggle to understand would confront Mary at every stage of her son's life. Parents of teenagers can identify with Mary when she and Joseph were separated from Jesus for three days, only to find him in the Temple. When Jesus explained that he had to be in his Father's house, Luke records, "they did not understand what he said to them." (Luke 2:50 NRSV). Perhaps by the time he was an adult, Mary understood better the enigmatic words of her son. But as a mother, did she understand when she and the brothers of Jesus, kept at a distance by a crowd, asked for him, only to hear that those who did the will of God were his brother and sister and mother (Mark 3:35)? Finally, in the Good Friday scenes portrayed in *The Passion* we see the culmination of Mary's struggle to understand.

Mary's life in relationship to Jesus is the story within the story of *The Passion*. It is the story of a mother's compassion that grew out of her fidelity to the word of God. Through her obedience to that word in the face of confusion, anxiety, and doubt, Mary came to be the great source of compassion Catholics and non-Catholic have always found her to be. That is why so many identify with her. And, what's more, we believe Mary's compassion did not end with death. This feast is an affirmation of our belief that Mary continues to be the companion of all who struggle to understand. Mothers, fathers, all who care deeply about others, can find in Mary a model of faith, and a constant source of comfort and consolation.

Questions for Further Discussion:

1. Do you think of Mary as a companion to those who suffer?
2. Have you experienced Mary's compassion in your life?

51
MARY OF THE DESERT
Feast of the Assumption (A)

- Revelation 11:19a; 12:1–6a, 10ab
- 1 Corinthians 15:20–27
- Luke 1:39–56

In his book, *Seeds of Contemplation,* Thomas Merton says about Mary:

> All that has been written about the Virgin Mother of God proves to me that hers is the most hidden of sanctities. What people find to say about her generally tells us more about their own selves than it does about our Lady.[17]

He then goes on to write many beautiful things about Mary, both in prose and poetry, which tell us much about Thomas Merton. But I think he is right. I suspect that if I were to ask any one of you today what Mary means to you, each would have a slightly different response. And each response would say something about the person responding. That being the case, it goes without saying that my reflections on Mary will also reveal something about myself. So be it.

My central thought about Mary comes from one of the lines in the first reading, the Book of Revelation, a reading which we believe symbolizes Mary. My favorite line from that reading is the line: "The woman herself fled into the desert where she had a place prepared by

God" (Rev 12:6). I am drawn to that line because it reminds me of Mary's solitude, her hiddenness, her way of disappearing, and reappearing when and where we may not expect her. But her disappearing into the desert is always consistent with her role in salvation history. She disappears, it seems, so that Christ might more fully appear. That to me is always the way Mary does things: When those who seek Christ find Mary in the desert, she always points them in the direction of Christ.

What is the desert where we find Mary? It is the place of prayer and contemplation each one of us eventually finds. It may be deep in the woods, high on a mountain, or in a side chapel before a statue of the Virgin. It may be found in the soothing recitation of the rosary, in the *Memorare*, or in the *Salve Regina*. Wherever hearts turn to prayer in the solitude and silence symbolized by the desert, Mary is there. And whether that prayer takes the form of words in praise of Mary, or words of intercession, she leads the seeker to her son.

What I have said is better expressed in Church teaching. When the college of bishops gathered in Rome for the Second Vatican Council in 1962, one of the issues before the council was whether to create a separate document concerned only with Mary. Wisely, those gathered in Rome recognized the danger of isolating Catholic teaching on Mary from the main doctrines of the council. They chose, instead, to include a chapter on the Blessed Virgin in *Lumen gentium* (the Constitution on the Church). That chapter includes this succinct statement:

> The maternal duty of Mary toward men in no way obscures or diminishes this unique mediation of Christ, but rather shows its power. For all the saving influences of the Blessed Virgin on men originate, not from some inner necessity, but from the divine pleasure. They flow forth from the superabundance of the merits of Christ, rest on His mediation, depend entirely on it, and draw all their power from it. In no way do they impede the immediate union of the faithful with Christ. Rather, they foster this union.[18]

What the council expressed in doctrine many have known through experience, myself included. Coming from a Protestant tradition that largely ignored Mary, except at Christmas when she appeared with Joseph in a nativity scene, all the stories of appearances, special prayers, and forms of devotion to Mary cascaded into my maturing consciousness like a surplus of wealth. Mary was a fascinating figure for me, a radically different religious person who suited my taste for newness just fine. I fell in love with Mary, there in the desert solitude of rural North Dakota. But then it seemed Mary fled again, perhaps deeper into the desert. But she did not flee until she had pointed me more directly to her son.

Now, on this feast of the Assumption, it would seem that Mary has fled this earth for "a place prepared by God." But, of course, we know that she only *seems* to have disappeared. While her home now is in heaven, we know Mary is not a stay-at-home kind of saint. When St. Thérèse of Lisieux prayed that she might spend her heaven doing good on earth, she was expressing a Marian theme. Mary spends her heaven appearing and reappearing in the world, but, most importantly, appearing in the desert spaces of people's lives. Today, we rejoice in knowing that Mary *is* present in our lives, pointing us to Christ.

Questions for Further Discussion:

1. Where has Mary appeared in your life? Has she disappeared, only to reappear in some new way?
2. Does Mary point you to her son, Jesus Christ?

52
I AM THE VOICE OF THE CAANANITE WOMAN[19]
Twentieth Sunday in Ordinary Time (A)

- Isaiah 56:1, 6–7
- Romans 11:13–15, 29–32
- Matthew 15:21–28

I am the voice of the Canaanite woman.

I have no name, no history; not much is written about me.

But I have a voice. My voice shaped the course of salvation history.

My voice was heard by Mark and Matthew, who dared write down my words, dared to record how I challenged their holy man, Jesus of Nazareth, and influenced the course of his mission.

I am the voice of the Canaanite woman.

I had to raise my voice to be heard that day. I had to shout at him, so great was the distance between us. Me, a Gentile woman, and him, Jesus of Nazareth, a Galilean Jew.

My voice carried across the great divide between us: "Have mercy on me, Lord. My daughter is tormented by a demon."

Yes, I called him "Lord, Son of David," for I knew who he was. And I knew what he could do, if he only would.

At first, he pretended not to hear me. And I know why. A woman? Speaking to a man in public?

Not done. Not a Gentile woman, speaking to a Jewish man,

Ah, the sheer *chutzpah* I felt that day!

I a Gentile; he a Jew. You see, his people looked down on my people. Called us dogs. This one was no different. It did not bother me. He was human after all. Dogs! No more than a figure of speech.

But my voice would not be silenced. Nothing would silence my voice—

not gender,
not ethnic difference,
not socioeconomics,
not politics,
not culture.

I would not be silent.

I am the voice of the Canaanite woman.

Those around him grew tired of my voice. They wanted to exclude me. He spoke of being sent "only to the lost sheep of Israel."

Even then I persisted.

You may ask what kept my voice from faltering? Why did I persist?

One word: *mercy.*

I knew him as a man of great mercy.

When he made that remark about not taking the food of children and throwing it to the dogs, I saw my chance. I knew about dogs. I knew that Jews regarded dogs that roamed the streets, scavenging for scraps, as unclean.

But I knew another kind of dog. I knew about the little dogs that sat beneath my table, household pets, who ate the small scraps that fell to them when my children ate. I knew mercy from my daily household experience.

And so when he said "dogs," I thought, "little puppies," those humble pets who receive mercy at my table.

When I said, "Please, Lord, for even the dogs eat the scraps that fall from the table of their masters," I knew my voice had prevailed.

His defenses crumbled. It was as though he had seen something he had not seen before. He seemed to suddenly be aware that his mercy did not have to be confined by gender, or ethnicity, or socio-economic boundaries. My humble experience of household mercy had touched his heart. He could not resist me.

He used a word to describe my faith that does not appear anywhere else in your Gospel. He said, "O woman, great is your faith!"

Great. That is the word he used to describe my faith.

But as he said those words, I whispered to myself, "And great is your mercy, Lord, for now it extends to all people, not just to the lost sheep of the house of Israel."

I know he was thinking that, because when he left there he went to the Sea of Galilee, which was where many Gentiles lived. There he healed many people and, as Matthew says, "they praised the God of Israel" (Matt 15:31 NRSV).

Those were my people, the Gentiles, who praised the God of Israel. And they received mercy, because my voice had changed Jesus of Nazareth. My voice challenged him, stretched him, deepened him, broadened his mission to Gentiles, not just Jews.

I am the voice of the Canaanite woman. And my voice cannot be silenced.

My voice can still be heard across the divide that separates the powerless, the weak, all those excluded from the mercy of Christ.

When a Palestinian mother weeps for her children, dying because of politics, my voice is raised in a plea for mercy.

When a Mexican-American woman weeps because her children know boredom, frustration, and eventually the violence of gangs, my voice pleads for mercy.

When a welfare mother is homeless,
because she cannot pay her rent,
because her welfare check was spent to fix her car,
because she must work to keep her welfare check,
and she needs her car to get to work,
my voice begs for mercy.

Wherever there are persons excluded from mercy, my voice will be heard.

I am the voice of the Canaanite woman.

Questions for Further Discussion:

1. Do you think that the voice of the Canaanite woman affected Jesus' mission?

2. Where do you hear the voice of the Canaanite woman today?

53

THE KEYS TO THE KINGDOM
Twenty-first Sunday in Ordinary Time (A)

- Isaiah 22:19–23
- Romans 11:33–36
- Matthew 16:13–20

In light of today's Gospel, I have to point out what appears to be an inaccuracy in one of the stained-glass windows here in our parish church. If you look up at the stained-glass window depicting St. Peter, to my right, your left, you will notice he is holding one big key. The question that occurs to me is: Where are the other keys? Matthew records Jesus as saying, "I will give you the keys to the kingdom of heaven" (16:19).

So, where are the other keys?

I have looked carefully at that window and cannot see any other keys. Are they hidden in Peter's pocket? Did he leave them back along the trail somewhere?

Where are the other keys?

You may have your opinions about how to solve this mystery. But let me suggest where I think the other keys are. The keys are scattered along the path leading to the kingdom of heaven. As we walk that path, the keys to our salvation are there for us, although often they may at times seem hidden. Our journey to the kingdom is a moment-by-moment search for the keys given to St. Peter and miraculously shared with us.

Our Church is built on the Rock of Peter and it is through the sacraments that the keys to the kingdom of heaven are given to us. Starting with baptism, all the way through to our final anointing, the keys to the kingdom of heaven are being placed in our hands. Our task is simply to recognize them and use them wisely.

Sometimes we think that the kingdom of heaven lies at the end of a long earthly journey, during which we endure trials and suffering, hoping that at long last St. Peter will unlock the gates of heaven for us. Although that may be true in a sense, we are also passing through the doors to the kingdom every day, if we recognize and use the keys given us.

If there were enough time, I could tell you how the keys given to St. Peter are present in each of the sacraments. But let me just focus on one sacrament, the sacrament of matrimony, to illustrate my point. I often say to young couples preparing for marriage that their call to the married life is a vocation, just like any other vocation, whether it be priesthood, religious life, diaconate, or single life. Each is a distinct call from God; with each vocation comes hundreds, no, *thousands,* of keys intended by God to bring us into the kingdom of heaven.

When a couple is called to the married life, it is the vocation willed by God for their salvation. No other vocation can bring them to the full glory of God. When a couple, standing before this altar, makes their vows to each other, they exchange rings. But they really should be exchanging keys, symbolizing the many keys to the kingdom of heaven that await them.

The first key given them is a deep, passionate, love for each other. It is a key that burns red hot and opens the door to unity. Through the wonderful gifts nature has provided, the couple uses this key to move out of themselves and into a deep, penetrating, caring relationship with the other. It is a door they pass through easily and with great pleasure.

But the key given at the start of the sacrament of matrimony, like the keys given to St. Peter, both opens and closes. It unlocks and locks up. It unlocks a passionate love but it also must lock the door to self-ishness, to old habits, to all the things that must be left behind if the couple is to journey well on the path of marriage. And yet, at the same time, it must not lock away the past so tightly that the marriage becomes stifling, smothering. The key must be used wisely. Couples who flour-ish in their marriage have learned to lock away all self-centeredness, while leaving wide open the individual uniqueness and interests of each partner.

On the marriage journey, just as with other vocations, there are keys that open doors better left closed. These are the illusory doors of affluence, of consumerism, secular values, of keeping up a lifestyle that leaves little time or energy for God. These doors promise a quicker route to happiness; but the key of wisdom will not open them.

I remember after my mother's death, how my stepfather, looking back over more than forty years of marriage, said, "We were happiest when we had nothing and were working hard just to get by." That is a key of wisdom many married couples here this morning know very well. It is a key that must be shared with those just starting out on the journey. We as a Church need to do more to bring that wisdom to those who need it.

It takes deep faith and trust in God to pick up many of the keys found along the married path. One of the doors through which most couples will pass bears this sign: CHILDREN. The key that opens this door is made of patience, courage, self-sacrifice. It is a key that will open up an entirely new and gratifying life for couples that pick it up. It is a key that for many will open the door to a deeper maturity.

There are many keys along the married path. And I leave it to your imagination to name them. I will mention only one other important key—the key of prayer. The simple wisdom still applies: "The family that prays together, stays together." I hear from many starting out on the path of marriage that they desire this key but often do not know where to find it. We need to do more to make this key available, for it leads through a door that promises the clearest view of the kingdom of heaven. What begins for a couple as simple shared prayer at meals can lead through the door to prayer over scripture, regular morning and evening prayer, silent prayer, and on and on, until the door of contemplation is reached.

Father Mike Winterer in talking about contemplative prayer uses this example: Picture an old couple, he says. They have been married for many, many years. They have reached the point where they are content just to sit quietly with each other. One day they are sitting quietly together and the man says to his wife, "I love you." And she says, "Shut up. You ruined it." The key of prayer will lead to that kind of unity that is as close as we can get to the experience of God in this life.

No matter what vocation we choose, there comes a time when we reach the final door—the door that leads to the next life. The key that opens this door is a strange alloy of sadness and joy. But if we have been faithful in accepting the keys along the path we have chosen, then this key will fit naturally into our hands. And the lock it fits will open easily.

When the final door is opened, perhaps we may see St. Peter standing with his big key. But he never has to use it. All of the little keys along the way have opened the door to heaven. We simply pass through.

Questions for Further Discussion:

1. Which of the keys mentioned is the most difficult to pick up?
2. What are some doors in your life you would like to find a key to open?

54
THE SATAN IN EACH OF US
Twenty-second Sunday in Ordinary Time (A)

- Jeremiah 20:7–9
- Romans 12:1–2
- Matthew 19:21–27

What is in a name?

Quite a bit, it seems.

Ask the people of Devils Lake, North Dakota. Ask Simon Peter.

If you follow the news from North Dakota—which, I suppose, most of you don't—you may have heard that Devils Lake High School recently voted to drop the name *Satans* from its sports teams. After eighty years it will no longer be the Devils Lake Satans. Being called Satan has become too controversial in these times of satanic cults and all that goes with them.

What is in a name?

Last week Peter was named the Rock; this week he is named "Satan, the Obstacle."

Satan is not a name most of us would want to be called, especially by Jesus. And yet, if we understand the history of the word *Satan,* we may find new insight into the message of this Gospel passage.

It must have been shocking to Peter to hear the name *Satan* applied to him. It certainly shocks us today. But it appears Peter did not overreact to this sharp language. He didn't drop out of disciple formation, he didn't quit the apostles, he didn't feel sorry for himself.

Why didn't Peter overreact to being called Satan that day on the trail to Jerusalem? I suspect it was because Peter did not see Jesus' choice of words as a put-down but, rather, as an important key to understanding and entering into the paschal mystery.

Peter had a better understanding of the term *Satan* than we have today. If Peter knew his Hebrew scriptures, he would have known that he was not the first person to be referred to as Satan. In fact, he was in pretty good company. The first person called a *satan* in the Old Testament is David.[20] In his early days, David had been a guerrilla leader who even joined forces with Philistines to overthrow Saul, who was then king of Israel. The Book of Samuel records the Philistines questioning whether to allow David to join them, because in time he might become a satan, an "adversary." A number of other passages in the Old Testament use the term *satan* to mean an adversary, someone who is a rival or opponent. If we think of Satan in this way, as an adversary or opponent, then the decision by Devils Lake High School to drop the name from their athletic teams seems ill-advised.

In later rabbinic sources, the term *Satan* is "identified in a more impersonal way with the evil inclination which infects humanity."[21] Thus, Satan is the source behind God's testing of Abraham, he is responsible for the Israelites worshiping the golden calf, and he is the force behind King David's sin with Bathsheba.

This background puts Jesus' statement in a different light. He was not saying Peter was Satan, in the sense of a celestial figure rivaling God in a contest between good and evil. He was not saying that Peter was possessed by Satan as we might think of that phenomenon after watching *The Exorcist*. Rather, Peter most likely understood Jesus to mean that he was being an adversary to Jesus and was giving in to a very human inclination to avoid pain and suffering at all costs.

That Jesus had this in mind is indicated by the words that follow when he says, "You are thinking not as God does, but as human beings do" (Matt 16:23). In other words, Peter's reaction came from a very human inclination that was adverse to God's way.

This understanding helps us because we have the same human inclination that got Peter into trouble. We have heard it preached many times that it was necessary for Jesus to go to Jerusalem, to suffer greatly, be killed and be raised again on the third day. And if we are honest with ourselves, we have to admit we react in much the same way as Peter, "God forbid, Lord." Perhaps part of the reason Peter reacted as he did was because he sensed the implications for himself. He had just professed that this Jesus was the Christ, he had committed himself to following Jesus Christ, and, if that was what Jesus had to undergo, then was it not likely he might suffer a similar fate?

And ourselves? Do we not shy away from what Jesus is talking about because we sense that it has implications for us as well? The paschal mystery, which is what Jesus was introducing Peter to, gives us all pause. It has enormous implications for our lives. Our human inclination is to *avoid* pain and suffering, so why should we embrace such a teaching, even if it comes from someone we trust and love?

The paschal mystery is about crossing over from death to life. The followers of Christ came to see his life, death, and resurrection as *Pascha,* or Passover, a term associated with the liberation of Israel from slavery in Egypt. Jesus is the one who passed over from death to life, the Lamb whose blood was shed to liberate humankind from slavery to sin.

In truth there is a paschal mystery in each of our lives. We cannot avoid it. The words from the prophet Jeremiah are testimony to that. He says he was duped by God. He thought he could remain on the sidelines, an innocent bystander. But God did not let that happen. The fire of God's presence welled up within him.

The juxtapositioning of Jeremiah with today's Gospel points to a certain inevitability about the paschal mystery. Through the incarnation, we have all been enticed by God! Or as another translation has it, "Duped!" Indeed, the whole world has been duped. The paschal mystery cannot be eliminated from anyone's life, it cannot be avoided, it is inevitable; it smolders, flares, subsides, flames up again, slowly purges, and, in rare lives, bursts into an all-consuming fire. The fiery anguish of being transformed from death to life is present in every life. The difference for believing Christians is this: By our faith in Christ, by our love for him, we come to see that our own paschal mystery is somehow a part of the paschal mystery of Christ.

We know that the paschal mystery has to operate in our lives. We know that the suffering we often experience is from our very human inclination to avoid pain and suffering. We all could be called Satan. But we know that the paschal mystery is the way to real life. We come to know that the dying to our old self issues forth into a kind of life unimaginable to us before we decided to enter into the mystery. We come to know that there is a glory found in living the mystery that makes earthly glory pale in comparison.

It helps to know the meaning of words. Words, like sticks and stones, *can* break us. But the words of Jesus should never do that. Jesus knew Peter's humanity; he knows ours. We need not fear anything Jesus said, not even the name Satan.

Questions for Further Discussion:

1. How do you think of Satan? As an adversary?
2. What does Jeremiah mean when he says he has been enticed (duped) by God?

55
CORRECTING THE SINNER
Twenty-third Sunday in Ordinary Time (A)

- Ezekiel 33:7–9
- Romans 13:8–10
- Matthew 18:15–20

You are a member of a small Catholic parish and are facing the following issues: (1) You serve on the liturgy committee and are becoming increasingly concerned with the way another member publicly criticizes the deacon about his preaching; (2) at Mass, you are frequently distracted by the poor quality of the flowers on the altar since Jane was put in charge of church ambience; (3) during the coffee hour, you sense that the choir director is becoming too familiar with the newly ordained priest recently assigned to the parish. What do you do?

Consult a doctor! Only, in this case, I do not mean a medical doctor, or even a doctor of theology. I have in mind a doctor of the Church. I have in mind St. Thérèse of Lisieux, declared a doctor of the Universal Church in the fall of 1997. St. Thérèse, the Little Flower, at one point in her life faced the same difficult issue we all face: how to correct the sinner? How to faithfully apply what Jesus says in today's Gospel: "If your brother sins against you, go and tell him his fault between you and him alone" (Matt 18:15). The way St. Thérèse applied this evangelical counsel can be helpful to each of us.

In his biography of St. Thérèse, *The Story of a Life: St. Thérèse of Lisieux,* Guy Gaucher, OCD, describes a difficult challenge Thérèse faced in her relationship with one of the members of her Carmelite community.[22] For some time she had been concerned about Sister Marthe's "inordinate attachment" to Mother Marie de Gonzague. At the risk of being betrayed, and even causing a conflict that might result in her being sent to another monastery, Thérèse, at the age of twenty, determined it was her duty to speak and not worry about the consequences. Her journal entries record that with great affection she counseled her fellow sister that it was the sacrifice of one's self, not attachment, that was needed. And it worked. Her biographer records that the "sisterly correction bore immediate fruit. Sister Marthe understood perfectly and would never forget that day of inner liberation."[23]

The example given by St. Thérèse is instructive for all of us here at St. Joseph Parish. We too encounter situations which we know call out for application of the evangelical counsel in today's Gospel. Unfortunately, we often fail to heed the advice Jesus gave his disciples. Our tendency is to do one of two things: (1) Do nothing, other than brood over the problem in secret, or (2) jump to the last option suggested by Jesus, that is, declaring the person, privately or publicly, the modern day equivalent of a "Gentile or a tax collector." Rather than approaching the offending person privately and with great affection, we default to an approach unlikely to produce a graced solution. The result is either an ongoing source of irritation or alienation from someone we are called to love as we do our own self.

Admittedly, our parish is far different from a Carmelite convent in nineteenth-century France, and none of us is a St. Thérèse. Still, we have something to learn from the doctor. First, her biographer mentions that she acted only after months of "patience and prayer." It takes patience to bear with someone who is annoying us but, unless we practice patience, we may not discern the approach demanded by the situation. Perhaps our perception of the other's behavior is skewed, perhaps we need more information or we need to step back for a minute. And certainly the evangelical counsel cannot be carried out well if we have not brought the problem into our prayer. Only when these two elements—patience and prayer—are operative can we expect to produce good fruit by our action.

It requires discipline to faithfully apply the mode of problem solving directed by today's Gospel, and demonstrated by St. Thérèse, because we are deeply conditioned culturally to approach problem solving in ways that are radically different from the Gospel ideal. One respected study of American culture identities individualism as the main characteristic of our American culture.[24] While this aspect of our culture has produced tremendous freedom and innovation, its dark side is a tendency toward isolation, the opposite of a loving community. Thus, we are prone to passivity in approaching community problems, provided they do not directly affect us. The Gospel directive challenges us to take responsibility for our neighbor in a loving manner.

At the other extreme is an aggressive approach to problem solving that also misses the mark set by the Gospel. You do not have to listen to many radio talk-show hosts, or be around many lawyers, to know what I mean. We are a society prone to aggressive, confrontational, litigious problem solving. Nowhere is this more painfully apparent than in our own Church and the sexual-abuse scandal that has plagued us. I am not suggesting that cases of sexual misconduct should not be confronted; I *am* saying that we all have to ask whether the evangelical counsel in today's Gospel could have been applied more faithfully at times.

Jesus certainly would have agreed with the prophet Ezekiel that we have a duty "to dissuade the wicked from his ways." He also would have agreed with Paul that the commandments are summed up in "You shall love your neighbor as yourself." But he also would have insisted that we can best put these sayings into practice by following the counsel he himself left us in today's Gospel. Go and live it!

Questions for Further Discussion:

1. Have you had to correct someone within the context of church? How did you go about it?

2. Have you acquired skills for problem solving from your education or work that would be useful in a church context?

56
RELEASING GOD'S MERCY TO THE WORLD
Twenty-fourth Sunday in Ordinary Time (A)

- Sirach 27:30—28:7
- Romans 14:7–9
- Matthew 18:21–35

Once there was a businessman who wanted to hire a new employee. The man devised a simple test for screening potential applicants for the job. He asked this simple question: How much is two plus two?

The first applicant was an accountant and, when he was asked the question, replied, "The answer is exactly 4.0."

The second applicant was an engineer and, before answering the question, the man applied several mathematical formulas, used his calculator, and replied, "The answer is 4.00193."

The third applicant was a lawyer. When asked, "How much is two plus two?" the lawyer thought for a moment and then asked, "How much do you want it to be?"

I would submit that the lawyer's response comes closer to the correct answer to the question raised in today's Gospel, "[H]ow often must I forgive?"

Peter's suggested answer—"as many as seven times"—is more like the answer given by the accountant and the engineer: a carefully calculated, definite, limited number. Had Peter been thinking more like a lawyer, he would have said, "What do you want the answer to be, Lord?" Jesus makes clear that the correct answer to the question—"How often must I forgive?"—implies an infinite number—"seventy-seven times." Other translations say, "seventy times seven." In other words, a very large number.

Our forgiving *has* to be *unlimited,* because God's mercy is *unlimited.* By forgiving without limit, we join in God's creative activity of bringing mercy to the world.

It is a joy to forgive from the heart. Note that I use the word *joy,* not *pleasure* or *fun.* Forgiving others is *not* a pleasurable activity. Indeed, it can be a hard, difficult, even painful thing to do. And yet the very clear message of the Gospel is that we must forgive from the heart. In my own experience, it seems that the best I can do is to forgive from the neck up. We make up our minds that we will forgive because we have heard the words from today's Gospel and do not want our Lord to hand us over to the torturers until we pay back our debt. What a grim prospect *that* is. But if we can forgive from the heart, it is a joy.

Forgiving others is not a sad task. It is joyful; not pleasurable, but joyful. Joyful, because in forgiving from the heart, we release God's mercy into a world badly in need of mercy. True forgiveness, the forgiveness that brings us joy, comes from the heart because that is where God is. In the deepest, innermost part of our being is where we find God.

Only God can forgive. We try with all that we have to forgive. But only God can forgive. When we tap into the divine pool of mercy, which is God dwelling in our hearts, then God's mercy flows out of us. It flows out to those around us, renewing relationships, creating small miracles, giving hope. Forgiveness, the releasing of God's mercy to the world, is something only we can do. God is dependent on us for this important task. Only God can forgive; only we can make it happen.

I recently came across a ritual of forgiveness that captures this truth that only God forgives. It is found in the Russian Orthodox tradition and is called Forgiveness Vespers. In this ritual, a person comes forward to the priest, makes a profound bow, and then asks forgiveness in these simple words, "Forgive me." The priest responds, "God forgives." Then, a kiss of peace is given. What a moving way to realize this profound truth that only God forgives!

How do we reach that pool of mercy God has placed in our hearts? How do we release God's mercy to the world? We do it by coming to realize that we ourselves are *always* in need of mercy. That involves honesty and humility. When we are self-righteous, when we persist in habits of judging or condemning others, then we lose the ability to see our own need for mercy. We can become obsessed with the speck in the other person's eye and forget the plank in our own. When we have the honesty to look at ourselves as God does, we see that the shortcomings of others are not much different from our own. Then it is that we are able to enter that part of our hearts where mercy is found. Then, we are able to release God's mercy to the world.

Joy is the proof that we have forgiven from the heart. When our forgiveness is less than that, we feel no joy. Whenever we forgive from the heart, we experience the kind of joy clouds must feel when they carry moisture to a parched land. When we forgive from the heart, our mercy drops, as Shakespeare says, "like the gentle rain from heaven," making it possible for new life to appear. Forgiving others is a divine act. And whenever we participate in divine activity, we experience joy.

In our post-9/11 world, there is perhaps no more important question than the one posed in today's Gospel—How often must I forgive? Sometimes the horrors we suffer seem too great to allow for forgiveness. But if we are able to see that we hold the key to unlocking God's mercy to our world, then our forgiving others takes on new meaning. We are the ones who will decide whether others will be healed by God's mercy or whether enmity and alienation will continue. God has placed in our hands a huge responsibility. Let us pray that we will respond generously.

Questions for Further Discussion:

1. What do you find difficult about forgiving others?
2. Do you believe that by forgiving others you release God's mercy to the world? In what way?

57
IT'S ALL ABOUT MERCY
Twenty-fifth Sunday in Ordinary Time (A)

- Isaiah 55:6–9
- Philippians 1:20c–24, 27a
- Matthew 20:1–16a

You cannot know a country, or a people, unless you know the stories. Not just know them, but internalize them, take them into the heart, let them change the way you see things, the way the world is experienced.

You cannot know Mexico without knowing about Moctezuma, about St. Juan Diego, the Blessed Virgin of Guadalupe. You cannot know Judaism without knowing the stories of the Hasidim, of the Baal Shem Tov. You cannot know Russia without knowing the stories of Dostoevsky and Tolstoy. You cannot know Ireland without knowing the stories of the Celts, of Patrick and Brennan…not to mention Yeats, Joyce, Shaw, and Beckett!

And you cannot know about the kingdom of heaven without knowing the stories of Jesus, the parables.

The stories Jesus told, like all of scripture, have a surplus of meaning. You cannot exhaust the meaning they contain. People of every age find something in these stories that speaks to them. When the followers of Jesus first heard the parable of the landowner and the laborers, its strange logic may have awakened them to how radically generous God had been with them. Certainly, those on the margins—the tax collectors and prostitutes—who it seems were welcomed more warmly than Pharisees, must have identified easily with the late-arriving laborers who got the usual wage—God's mercy. Later, when the author of Matthew wrote this Gospel for a largely Hebrew audience, the parable may have provoked the thought that Gentiles had an equal claim to God's mercy, even though they had not toiled in the vineyard planted by Abraham.

The Gospel text has been heard in many different tongues, many different contexts, but always the message is the same: God is radically generous; so generous, it is difficult for us to comprehend. Jesus understood this difficulty and did not try to proclaim the reality of God's mercy in abstract terms; only in story was it possible for this truth to work its way into the consciousness of people who, like ourselves, labored under a limited understanding of God's love.

Jesus begins his story with these words, "The kingdom of heaven is like...." Whenever we hear these words, we need to wake up, be alert, pay attention, for we are going to hear a story that is foreign to us. Jesus does not seem to have told stories simply to delight his listeners. (At least the gospel writers didn't record any). The stories Jesus tells always have a point to them. They always tend to perplex us, perhaps confuse us, for they seem to go against the grain of what we take for granted. And perhaps that is why Jesus told this story—to *upset* us and thereby start us thinking more deeply about what the kingdom of heaven is all about.

We have some warning in today's readings that the kingdom will seem strange to us. Isaiah says in the first reading, "For my thoughts are not your thoughts, nor are your ways my ways, says the LORD" (55:8). We should know that the kingdom is something radically different, something beyond our ordinary concepts and patterns of thinking. To relate to the kingdom, we must, in a sense, abandon our customary way of thinking. Our ideas about fairness in the workplace no longer apply. Thoughts like "A day's pay for a day's work" must be left behind. On the level of our ordinary existence, these concepts do, indeed, apply; in the kingdom of heaven they do not.

Of course, Jesus is *not* suggesting that in our everyday world a worker should *not* be paid a fair wage. To draw that conclusion would be a great misunderstanding. No, the story is intended as a way of shocking us into realizing that when it comes to life in Christ, life in the kingdom, God is radically generous and will shower down mercy whenever and wherever God wants. The purpose of the parable is to wake us up to this fact.

One of our human weaknesses is thinking that God behaves just the way we do. This weakness disposes us to think that our ordinary attitudes developed in the working world should apply when it comes to understanding the kingdom of heaven. We are taught in the working world to be competitive, to be always mindful of our own self-interest, to be efficient. We carry over into our understanding of God the false notion that God is stingy, that God's mercy is scarce, hard to come by. Almost unconsciously, we project these characteristics onto God. If we are not careful, we can come to think that God expects us to slavishly earn merit in God's eyes, much the way we earn a paycheck. This is heresy, an illusion that keeps us from experiencing the kingdom of heaven. Our relationship with God is not like a "bank account" where we accumulate grace that can be cashed in at the end of the day. The story teaches us that God's grace, God's mercy, is given lavishly, indiscriminately, extravagantly, inefficiently, not according to our ordinary notions but according to the supraordinary generosity and providence of God.

We have all been given some insight into this mystery through our own ordinary experience. Who among us has not at some point in his or her life experienced some undeserved, unexpected mercy, perhaps through parents, teachers, a friend. Perhaps in prayer we have had that experience where, in the honesty of our hearts, we admit, "I didn't deserve that mercy. I didn't work for it. It just fell from the sky, 'like the gentle rain.'" Why then should we be shocked if God shows the same generosity, but to the nth degree, to those who enter the kingdom?

I can find no better expression of this truth than what the great Carmelite poet, Jessica Powers, captured in her poem, "The Mercy of God,"[25] where she writes:

> I am copying down in a book from my heart's archives
> the day that I ceased to fear God with a shadowy fear.
> Would you name it the day that I measured my column of
> virtue
> and sighted through windows of merit a crown that was
> near?
> Ah, no, it was rather the day I began to see truly
> that I came forth from nothing and ever toward nothing-
> ness tend,
> that the works of my hands are a foolishness wrought in
> the presence
> of the worthiest king in a kingdom that never shall end.

The poet knows what all saints and mystics have come to know on their journey to the kingdom: It is all about *mercy*.

Questions for Further Discussion:

1. When have you experienced mercy? From God? From others?
2. When have you shown mercy?

58
JESUS THE RADICAL TEACHER
Twenty-sixth Sunday in Ordinary Time (A)

- Ezekiel 18:25–28
- Philippians 2:1–11
- Matthew 21:28–32

Sometimes, something as ordinary as reading the letters to the editor can help us understand the Kingdom of God.

Several weeks ago, someone wrote a letter to the editor of the Ogden [Utah] *Standard Examiner* complaining that the Weber County Library permits the homeless to use that facility as their "living quarters." The writer complained that the homeless are dirty, often smell bad, and that the library "chooses to treat these tramps as equal to the rest of us citizens."

It was heartening to read the responses to this letter. A handful of letters appeared criticizing the writer's dim view of the homeless. One woman described how her own son, afflicted with mental illness, had once been homeless and had frequented the library, but how, thanks to medical intervention, had been returned to better health. She reminded readers of that old saying, "But for the grace of God, there go I." Another wrote, reminding readers that the homeless we see in the library are "human beings with thoughts and feelings, desires and needs, and they are just as valuable on this planet as you and I are."

Without using religious language, these writers captured something we heard in today's second reading from Philippians. Paul talks about the attitude of Christ, who, "though he was in the form of God, did not regard equality with God something to be grasped. Rather, he emptied himself, taking the form of a slave, coming in human likeness" (2:6).

In contemporary terms, we might say that Christ humbled himself and took the form of a homeless person. After all, Christ says elsewhere in the gospel, "Foxes have holes, and birds of the air have nests; but the Son of Man has nowhere to lay his head" (Luke 9:58 NRSV). Jesus lived much like a homeless person. And I am sure after walking those hot, dusty trails of Galilee, roads where donkeys and other animals had passed, he must have smelled at times much like the homeless man sitting in the Weber County Library. Certainly, Jesus was closer in appearance to the homeless than to the wealthy members of his society.

Without even mentioning their inherent value as children of God, the homeless play a valuable role in reminding us that Christ is present among us in the poor. Blessed Mother Teresa once said that Christ is present in the world in the terrible disguise of the poor.

But the homeless not only represent Christ the poor man; they play another valuable role for us—they remind us of Christ the Radical Teacher. They are modern-day, living reminders of how we come to enter the Kingdom of God.

Let us leave for a moment the homeless man sitting quietly in the Weber County Library and journey back two-thousand years to the scene presented in today's Gospel. Once again, Jesus is engaged in a debate with the chief priests and elders of the people who have been trying to catch him in carefully set traps. Here we see an example of Christ the Radical Teacher.

Jesus has just foiled these learned men by asking them where John the Baptist's authority came from—human or divine—and they were unable to give a reply. Now, he says something that must have shaken them to their roots. He says, "[T]ax collectors and prostitutes are entering the kingdom of God before you" (Matt 21:31). To the chief priests and elders, this group of people—tax collectors and prostitutes—was probably as despised as the homeless are in our society today. Were Jesus speaking today, he might say, "the homeless are entering the kingdom of God before you."

Why did Jesus use such a radical contrasting? Why would a despised group of people be more likely to respond to Christ than men who had spent their lives in religious study and practice?

It has to do with attitude. The despised people at the time of Jesus had nothing to lose; they were not clinging to anything—not their wealth, not their pride, not their privileged position in society. Their attitude was closer to that of Christ: an attitude of detachment, because they had nothing. The despised ones were freer to enter into a relationship with Christ than were the Jewish authorities who had so much to lose by responding to this itinerant preacher from Galilee. They had all their learning, their positions of respect and privilege in the Temple, they had their comfortable lives. Theirs was an attitude of radical attachment—attachment to all the things they had worked so hard to obtain and could not let go of—not even when the God they claimed to serve was standing right in front of them.

And so Jesus gives them the parable of the two sons. He is saying to them in words they clearly understood that the tax collectors and prostitutes who, by their actions, appeared to have rejected God's will ended up by doing it, since they had heeded the words of John the Baptist and had followed Jesus. The Jewish authorities, on the other hand, had declared from the start that they would do God's will—but when the Word of God came among them, they would not listen to him. That was Jesus the Radical Teacher at his best. No wonder they hated him!

But the parable is not limited in its application to the Jewish authorities. Like all of scripture, it applies as well to us. Let us return to the homeless man seated in the Weber County Library.

Part of the homeless person's value is in reminding us that we still have a long way to go in responding to the gospel message of Jesus. The homeless man may never have declared himself a follower of Christ; but by living with so little, by living without the security of wealth, or prestige, or power, the homeless man models the way of Christ and may, like the tax collectors and prostitutes, be going into the Kingdom of God ahead of any one of us. The homeless remind us of Christ the Radical Teacher.

This is not to suggest that we must become homeless in order to enter the Kingdom of God, nor is it meant to romanticize the life of the homeless, which can be terribly harsh. Jesus had devoted followers who were wealthy and who held positions of influence. It is simply to suggest another reason for treating the homeless with respect: They are the ones chosen by Christ the Radical Teacher to teach us the way to a deeper, more meaningful relationship with God through Christ. They remind us of our own need to become more aware of the gospel.

Jesus loved the chief priests and elders as much as he did tax collectors and prostitutes; he wanted to embrace them as children of his Father. But he knew that sometimes it takes a disturbing example to awaken someone to the Truth. Perhaps we too need to be awakened so we may enter more fully into the Kingdom of God.

Questions for Further Discussion:

1. Do you agree that the homeless have something important to teach us? What would it be?

2. Why might the homeless be going into the Kingdom of God ahead of us?

59
THE DIVINE LANDOWNER AND THE FOOLISH TENANTS: A PLAY IN THREE ACTS
Twenty-seventh Sunday in Ordinary Time (A)

- Isaiah 5:1–7
- Philippians 4:6–9
- Matthew 21:33–43

The Gospel of Matthew is packed with drama; today's parable is but one example. Jesus had a keen sense of the dramatic.

The parable we just heard is a trilogy, a play in three acts, a drama that stretches back to the time of Abraham and Moses and forward into eternity. As followers of Christ, we play an important role in that great drama.

You may ask, "What kind of play is this? Is it a tragedy? A comedy?" No, neither of these. It is a love story!

It is a story of love offered, and love rejected. It is a tale of a faithful lover who loves creation, and longs to be loved in return. It is a drama of the Divine Landowner and the foolish tenants, children of God, created to be loved and to return love, who are out of relationship with God. And it is about servants sent by God to restore that loving relationship.

Here is a synopsis of the first two acts of this three-act play. Act one is set in ancient Israel. As the scenes unfold, we see God establishing a radically new relationship of love with the people of Israel—a covenant of love, first with Noah, then with Abraham, and finally, through Moses, a covenant with the people of Israel. It is a covenant wherein God says to the people of Israel: I will make with you a covenant that no other people can claim. I will be your God and you will be my people. Within that covenant, God's love would be constant and the people would flourish in a land flowing with milk and honey, a land as rich and fruitful as the vineyard in the parable.

But we know what happened. The people forgot the covenant; they turned away from God and substituted foreign gods, idols; they neglected the poor and the stranger. To bring them back, God sent the prophets to warn them, to cajole them, even to threaten them. God sent the prophets, like the servants in the parable, to collect what was rightfully due the Divine Landowner—the return of love from those who were the beneficiaries of love. But the prophets, like the servants, were uniformly rejected and mistreated. Jeremiah was even thrown into a dry well. Though they spoke for God, each of the servant-prophets experienced rejection.

The second act of this play is also familiar to us. In this act, it is Jesus who is sent to the people of Israel to receive what was rightfully owing to God—the love of God's people. Everything Jesus did in his public ministry—the preaching, the miracles, the healing—all was intended to win back the love of the foolish tenants. But we know what happened. We know how the second act ends: Once again the servant, who was God Incarnate, was rejected like the servants who went before him. Not only rejected; this Suffering Servant was betrayed, tortured, and killed. As the curtain falls on the second act, picture the cross dominating the scene.

Now we come to the third act. Again, it is servants who play the leading role. But in this act, it is not the prophets of old who have the main role. It is you and I. We are now the servants sent by God to deliver to the Divine Landlord all the love, the devotion, the commitment that is owing. Each of us here today—priest, deacon, religious, layperson—each of us is a ministering servant. And I suppose at times we feel as rejected as the servants in the first act. The people we are sent to minister to do not appreciate us. We find ourselves unable to awaken in the tenants that excitement about God we had hoped to find when we first became servants.

But as we carry out our role as servants in this third act, there is something we must keep in mind—Christ is with us. You have probably seen plays where one actor appears in more than one scene. That is the case with us. At the end of the second act, it seemed to the foolish that Jesus, the Servant of God, was gone from the drama. It seemed that the curtain had fallen on his presence and he would not be seen again. But those who are able to see with the eyes of faith experience something marvelous, something tremendous—Jesus is present in the third act as well. And that is our task, fellow servants, to minister in such a way that those who see us, see Jesus Christ as well.

How then do we reveal that it is Christ the Servant acting in and through us? We do it by supporting one another. No servant can minister well alone. We need the support of other servants. We need the support of this community as it celebrates the Eucharist; we need the support of small Christian communities; we need the support of our families, strengthened by prayer, by scripture study, by retreats. Without that ongoing support, people will not recognize Jesus the Servant in us.

There are many kinds of plays and many different endings. Those who saw only the first two acts of this play might think that it is a tragedy. After all, the main characters die. But we know the play did not end with the second act. We know that this act, the third and final act, is where the story will be played out. And what's more, we know through faith that the ending will be glorious. The play is not a tragedy. It is the story of salvation and it will continue until it merges into eternity.

My friends, we have an important role to play as servants. Let us pray that we will play our parts well.

Questions for Further Discussion:

1. Can you picture yourself as a player in this great drama of salvation? What role do you play?

2. What does it mean that Jesus appears in the third act of this drama as well?

60
ENJOY THE PARTY!
Twenty-eighth Sunday in Ordinary Time (A)

- Isaiah 25:6–10a
- Philippians 4:12–14, 19–20
- Matthew 22:1–14

Sometimes even fictional characters can help open up the gospel for us. For today's Gospel parable, I have turned to someone you may not have heard of—the Little Prince. A Frenchman, Antoine de St. Exupéry, has left us a delightful little book called *The Little Prince*.[26]

Although he comes from another planet the size of a house, the Little Prince has the marvelous ability to see what is essential in life. One of his best insights comes from a dialogue he has with a fox, whom he has tamed. The wisdom he has gained from the fox is this: "It is only with the heart that one can see rightly; what is essential is invisible to the eye."[27]

This little bit of wisdom helps us see what is essential in today's parable. What is essential is joy, mercy, hope, and freedom.

At first blush, you might think that the parable we just heard has nothing to do with joy, mercy, hope, and freedom. When we look at it with our ordinary eyes, we see invited guests who refuse a great feast, guests who greet the invitation with violence, guests described as not worthy, and even a man turned away because he wore the wrong clothes!

Where is the message of joy, mercy, hope, freedom in all this? But, remember: "What is essential is invisible to the eye."

When we look with the eye of the heart we see, first of all, that the kingdom of heaven is a joyous event. The kingdom is like a big party, *una fiesta grande*, a big, fat Jewish wedding party! Jesus says the kingdom of heaven is like a big wedding feast, whether it be Jewish, Greek, or even (as in the case of *Babette's Feast*) Scandinavian. That is exciting news, a cause for great joy. Our gathering here today for Eucharist is but a sampling of that joy, a warm-up, a preparty event.

But there is more that is essential in this vision of the kingdom. There is a golden nugget of mercy in this parable that, despite its brightness, might not be easily seen. It is hidden in the lines that talk about the hall being filled with guests, both good and bad alike. God has thrown open the party to people we might never expect to see there. They are there because of the mercy of God. They are there for reasons unknown to us.

Another Frenchman, Blaise Pascal, said, "The heart has its reasons that reason knows not of." We might go a step further and say, "The heart of God has its reasons that our reason knows not of." The mercy of God is not so much irrational as it is suprarational. It is part of the mystery of God. We cannot see it with our eyes; we can only experience it in our hearts.

Thomas Merton, an American born in France, said that God is mercy within mercy within mercy. One example comes to mind: the thief who was crucified on a cross next to Jesus. Do you think that anyone looking on that scene with ordinary eyes could have predicted that *this* man would that day be welcomed into the kingdom of heaven? The Little Prince reminds us that it is only with the heart we see things rightly. The Gospel is about second chances, third chances, chances ad infinitum. That is the hope in this parable.

And then we come to the freedom that this knowledge gives us. When we are able to see with the heart what is essential in the gospel we are free! Free from judging others; free from that wasteful habit of trying to sort out who is worthy and who is not, who will be in the kingdom and who will not be; free from that energy-draining fear that our loved ones will be turned away from the kingdom; free from the anxiety that haunts so many good parents when their equally good children drift away from the Catholic faith.

And so, if we are free from worrying about who will be worthy to attend the great feast in the kingdom of heaven, how should we spend our time? I would offer this simple advice: Enjoy the party!

No one would ever come to a celebration where the guests are all standing around looking gloomy, anxiously comparing notes as to who's there and who's not. No one would want to join a fiesta where, instead of dancing and singing, there were worried, judgmental people, begrudging the presence of "those people." People are attracted to people who are joyful, not worried, people who know how to enjoy a wedding feast.

We all want our loved ones to be with us at the wedding feast, especially our children. We must teach our children well, bring them to church all the time, pray like St. Monica did for St. Augustine when they stray. But when we have done all that, we should simply enjoy the party. I believe it was still another Frenchman, Pierre Teilhard de Chardin, who said that joy is the surest sign of the presence of God. Our joy, which is based on the firm foundation of hope in God's mercy, is what will bring our loved ones to the kingdom.

And so, my friends, enjoy the party!

Questions for Further Discussion:

1. Are you able to see with the heart? Most of the time? Some of the time?

2. What helps you to enjoy the party?

61
KEEP TO THE MIDDLE WAY
Twenty-ninth Sunday in Ordinary Time (A)

- Isaiah 45:1, 4–6
- 1 Thessalonians 1:1–5b
- Matthew 22:15–21

Once again, a dramatic gospel scene, a scene packed with meaning at many different levels. It is a scene rich in wisdom, a wisdom that can help us journey safely through this life into the Kingdom of God.

It is also a scene of clever trickery. Sharp-minded Pharisees and Herodians confront Jesus with a carefully crafted question, a question designed to lure Jesus away from the sacred middle way and place him in an extreme position that will hasten his destruction. If he says pay the tax, he will have acknowledged the sovereignty of Rome and offended his fellow Jews; if he says don't pay it, he might have been charged with sedition by the Romans.

The response Jesus gives reveals a wisdom both ancient and yet new. It is the wisdom of the golden mean, the "way of wisdom and safety between extremes," a way of keeping one's balance in all things. It is the middle way.

An ancient myth captures the wisdom of the middle way.

The Greeks gave us the myth of the skillful artificer, Daedalus, and his beloved son, Icarus. Imprisoned on an island by King Minos, whose favor he had lost, Daedalus plots his escape. Knowing he cannot escape by sea, Daedalus finds inspiration in the flight of birds and fabricates wings for himself and his young son, Icarus. Carefully, he crafts his wings, securing the larger feathers with thread and the smaller ones with wax. His work at last finished, Daedalus takes to the air, soaring with the freedom of a bird. He coaxes his son to follow him, and, as they prepare to escape the island, he gives Icarus this advice: "Icarus, my son, I charge you to keep at a moderate height, for if you fly too low the damp will clog your wings, and if too high the heat will melt them. Keep near me and you will be safe."[28] Daedalus knew the wisdom of the middle way.

With those instructions, Daedalus, his face wet with tears, kissed his boy, rose into the air on his beautiful wings, and flew toward freedom. The storyteller says that shepherds leaned on their staffs, plowmen ceased their labor, all stood in awe at the flight of Daedalus and Icarus.

But we know what happens. The boy, overcome with the excitement of his wings, soared higher and higher, as if to reach the heavens. He soared so high that the sun melted the wax that held the feathers together. Down he spiraled into the blue waters of the sea. His father cried, "Icarus, Icarus, where are you?" but found only feathers floating on the water. A poet expressed the tragedy of Icarus this way:

...with melting wax and loosened strings
Sunk hapless Icarus on unfaithful wings;
Headlong he rushed through affrighted air,
With limbs distorted and disheveled hair;
His scattered plumage danced upon the wave,

And sorrowing Nereids decked his watery grave;
O'er his pale corse their pearly sea-flowers shed,
And strewed with crimson moss his marble bed;
Struck in their coral towers the passing bell,
And wide in ocean tolled his echoing knell[29]

The temptation Jesus faced, the temptation we all face, is the temptation Daedalus warned his son against. It is the temptation to leave the middle way. The first temptation that threatens our safe journey to the kingdom comes simply from our being human. We have been blessed by God with so many material things, all of them *good:* food, recreation, sexuality, freedom to do as we please. Everything good that God has given us for our enjoyment can paradoxically be the very temptation that lures us from the middle way. The temptation is always there—to take the extreme way of material things to the exclusion of the spiritual.

Like the force of gravity tugging on poor Icarus, our culture pulls us toward a life of extreme material indulgence. Our consumer-oriented culture coaxes us to take the *lower* way, to indulge our every sensual desire, to consume and still fly freely. But wisdom reminds us we were made for higher flight. In the words of essayist, Annie Dillard, "A life of good days lived in the senses is not enough. The life of sensation is the life of greed; it requires more and more. The life of the spirit requires less and less; time is ample and its passage sweet."[30] The temptation for more and more gradually pulls us down to an extreme way that leaves us hovering dangerously close to the waves of destruction.

If our natural inclination to seek satisfaction in material things is the inevitable result of our being human, it is our natural longing for the higher reaches of existence that poses an equal threat. A part of us always longs for and seeks to possess the beautiful, the true, and the good. We are drawn like Icarus to the heavens above us. But here too there is danger in leaving the middle way. We are faced with the constant temptation to travel in a way that seems effortless, without cost, without pain. New Age spirituality, the occult, the drug culture all offer a false way to freedom. They offer the illusion of flying high in the heavens, but they lead ultimately to the merciless heat of the sun. And the stories of our times that come out of this ersatz religious culture are stories of destruction no worse than that of poor Icarus. As a society, we weep continually at the sites where those who have left the middle way and flown too near the sun have met their own destruction.

Christ *is* the middle way. Christ *is* the golden mean. Christ *is* the one who leads the world safely through the twin dangers that lie in wait at the extremes. Christ is especially well suited to lead us along the middle way, for he stands between humanity and God. Jesus walked the middle way all through his ministry. Jesus knew the extreme temptations of the material world as well as the spiritual. Jesus walked the middle way and so must we.

In his time, Jesus guided his followers along the middle way. He continues to do so in our time. He does it through his Church. It is through the Church that we keep to the middle way. If you want to find proof of the wisdom of the middle way, study the history of your Church.

My friends, remember Icarus! Keep to the middle way!

Questions for Further Discussion:

1. How would you describe the ancient wisdom expressed in the myth of Icarus? Do you find it relevant to your life today?

2. Do you think the Catholic Church keeps to the middle way? Should it?

62
LAWYERS AND THE TEN COMMANDMENTS
Thirtieth Sunday in Ordinary Time (A)

- Exodus 22:20–26
- 1 Thessalonians 1:5c–10
- Matthew 22:34–40

Take it from me, a lawyer: Lawyers never change. Whether it's today, or whether it's the Gospel scene we just heard from Matthew, lawyers seem to have a knack for misunderstanding the Ten Commandments.

The Pharisee who questions Jesus is referred to as a lawyer, obviously sent to trip up Jesus. He was, perhaps, closer to being a canon lawyer than a civil lawyer, like myself, but a lawyer all the same. And like a good lawyer, he knew the letter of the law. But did he grasp its spirit?

Today, two-thousand years after the scene in Matthew's Gospel, lawyers are still doing the same thing—focusing on the letter of the

law, while missing the essence of the law that is to love without limitation, both God, self, and neighbor. Let me give you two examples.

First, an example very close to home. Ogden City recently lost a
case at the Tenth Circuit Court of Appeals involving its right to main-
tain a large monument of the Ten Commandments on municipal
grounds.[31] The case arose when a religion formed in 1975, called
"Summum," asked that a similar monument be erected displaying the
Seven Principles of the Summum religion. These principles include:
The Principle of Psychokinesis, the Principle of Correspondence, the
Principle of Vibration, the Principle of Opposition, the Principle of
Rhythm, the Principle of Cause and Effect, and the Principle of
Gender. Followers of Summum believe that these principles are the
keys to unlocking the Grand Principle of Creation. The court held
that the free-speech clause of the First Amendment compelled Ogden
City to treat with equal dignity speech from divergent religious per-
spectives; it could not allow the Ten Commandments monument without also displaying the Seven Principles Monument.

A second example, similar to Ogden's case, comes from the state
of Alabama where the chief justice of the supreme court, who ran for
election as the "Ten Commandments Judge," had a massive stone carv-
ing of the Ten Commandments placed in the rotunda of the state
supreme court building. The chief justice had the monument erected
to restore "those absolute standards that serve as the moral foundation
of law" and to "recognize the source from which all morality
springs…[by] recognizing the sovereignty of God." A federal court has
recently ruled that the monument must go.

It seems to me that if Jesus were on the scene today he would pro-
pose a solution to the controversy. His proposal would reflect what he
said to the Pharisee scholar of the law. He would say, "Forget the granite monuments, which no one pays much attention to anyway, and simply follow the heart of the law—'You shall love the Lord, your God,
with all your heart, with all your soul, and with all your mind'" (Matt
22:37). And he would add: "You shall love your neighbor as yourself."

Would this proposal satisfy the litigants in these cases? Perhaps
not.

It probably would not be accepted, because after two-thousand
years we still tend to think of the Ten Commandments as they were
described by the chief justice of the Alabama Supreme Court—"the ultimate source of morality." While in a highly qualified sense this is true, it
misses this important point: The commandment to love precedes the
Mosaic expression of the law found in the Ten Commandments.

Consider this Hasidic story, from a collection by Martin Buber, entitled "Keeping the Law."

> Disciples asked the maggid of Zlotchov: "In the Talmud we read that our Father Abraham kept all the laws. How could this be, since they had not yet been given to him?" "All that is needful," he said, "is to love God. If you are about to do something and you think it might lessen your love, then you will know it is sin. If you are about to do something and you think it will increase your love, you will know that your will is in keeping with the will of God. That is what Abraham did."[32]

What a marvelous restatement of what Jesus said in today's Gospel! Like the Gospel, it is filled with hope, for it expresses a religious understanding that predates the three great religions of the Book—Judaism, Christianity, and Islam. It is an expression of God's commandment to love that underlies all subsequent expressions of law.

The commandment to love is the essence of God's eternal covenant with Abraham. It is a relationship of love, not just between God and Abraham, but between God and all people who claim Abraham as their father in faith. The Ten Commandments, given to Moses at Mt. Sinai, were but a social expression of that covenant. They were intended to preserve the covenant, to create the conditions in which that unprecedented love could flourish. Following the maggid's advice to do only those things that increase your love does not obviate the need for the other commandments. As Jesus said, he did not come to do away with the commandments but to fulfill them. But it frees us from the divisive and counterproductive arguments over granite monuments, the separation of church and State, and…it avoids a lot of legal fees!

Monoliths of stone, granite monuments with the Ten Commandments carved on them, can ironically become idols, when what is needed is an *icon*. An idol is obtuse; it arrests the vision. The viewer's attention becomes fixed on the material thing and is not directed to truth. Icons, in contrast, are transparent, allowing the eye of the beholder to pass easily through to the truth they represent. Sadly, the monuments at issue in Ogden City and in Alabama are more like idols than icons—they do not draw the viewer to a deeper level where the great commandment to love is found.

We were blessed during the latter part of the twentieth century to have a living icon among us in the person of Blessed Mother Teresa of Calcutta. She never constructed granite monuments; instead, her life was a continual icon that expressed clearly the two great commandments Jesus articulated in the Gospel. Mother Teresa once said of the commandment to love: "[E]veryone can reach this love through meditation, spirit of prayer, and sacrifice, by an intense inner life."[33] These practices are not those of the lawyer but, rather, those of the saint.

At the end of the day, we cannot blame the lawyers for arguing over the Ten Commandments. In many ways, we are all lawyers when it comes to practicing our religion. What is needed are Catholics who are able to go deeper, to get beyond the surface to the heart of the matter. When we reach the ground of our being, we discover there the law of love. When we reach that level, we desire to do only those things that increase love. Then we are living the Ten Commandments.

Questions for Further Discussion:

1. Do you agree that in arguing over Ten Commandment monuments we have missed the essence of the law which is to love?

2. What is the difference between an idol and an icon?

63
ZEN MASTER BIRD'S NEST
Feast of All Saints (A)

- Revelation 7:2–4, 9–14
- 1 John 3:1–3
- Matthew 5:1–12a

On the feast of All Saints, we celebrate the "servants of our God," which St. John symbolized by the figure 144,000, representing the unlimited number of holy ones marked with the seal. When we hear that infinite number, we think not only of great saints but perhaps even lesser known ones, such as St. Simon Stylites whose unique ascetic practice was to sit at the top of a stone pillar for most of his years. Or perhaps even Zacchaeus, clinging to the branches of a sycamore tree as Jesus passed by. And when I think of those two, the name of someone from the Buddhist tradition comes to mind, a man who has something to teach us on this feast day. His name is Zen Master Bird's Nest.

Bird's Nest got his name from his practice of meditating in the branches of trees. One day when Bird's Nest was meditating in this fashion, the prime minister came along and shouted up into the tree, "Ahoy, Bird's Nest." Bird's Next shouted down, "Hey, there, Prime Minister." The prime minister said, "You look very unstable up there." Bird's Nest replied, "You look very unstable down *there*." The prime minister said, "Tell me, what is the essence of Zen?" Bird's Nest said, "Do good and avoid evil." The prime minister said, "Why, any five-year-old could have told me that." Bird's Nest said, "A five-year-old may be able to say it, but an eighty-year-old may be unable to do it."[34]

And that is what describes a saint. A saint is someone who at age eighty is able to do what he or she was able to say at age five. Sound simple? It *is* simple, because holiness is simple. We are the ones who make it complicated.

Holiness is as simple as the Beatitudes from Matthew's Gospel where we are told: Be poor, be meek, be merciful, be peacemakers. This way of living is so simple, a five-year-old could say it. But how many eighty-year-olds—fifty-year-olds? thirty-year-olds?—are able to do it? All Saints' Day is a good time to ask, "Why?"

Another Zen story offers insight into why we all have trouble doing what a five-year-old can say:

A Master saw a disciple who was very zealous in meditation. The Master said, "Virtuous one, what is your aim in practicing Zazen [meditation]?"

The disciple said: "My aim is to become a Buddha."

Then the Master picked up a tile and began to polish it on a stone in front of the hermitage.

The disciple said: "What is the Master doing?"

The Master said: "I am polishing this tile to make it a mirror."

The disciple said: "How can you make a mirror by polishing a tile?"

The Master replied: "How can you make a Buddha by practicing Zazen?"[35]

What does this say to us on the feast of All Saints? It says we will never become holy, never become saints, by our efforts alone. The Master was *not* saying that the disciple should give up meditation entirely, only that he should not think that meditation alone would bring him enlightenment anymore than polishing a tile could turn it into a mirror. We too may try to polish our souls through meditation, good works, disciplined living, but at some point we realize that holiness comes through surrendering to God. We cannot create a spotless mirror through our exterior practices. And even if we could produce such a spotless mirror and look into it, what would we see? Our own image, of course! That is not the way to holiness.

The way to holiness ultimately involves surrender and acceptance of who we are—children of God. When we surrender completely to God, we discover the real spotless mirror deep in our being. And what we see reflected there is the holiness of God. And in that reflection we recognize our own image, made in the likeness of God. The real key to holiness is remembering the dignity of our being and then living lives that are consistent with that dignity.

We are not tiles in need of polishing. We come to holiness through the mercy of Christ. And we come to holiness as a community of believers, each one a unique reflection of the great stream of Christ light that flows freely through the cosmos. It is in a community such as this one, a community made up of saints, big and small, each of them a companion on the journey, that we will arrive at the throne of God. It is in community that we learn to do the simple things any five-year-old could say: Make peace with that person in the parish you have been squabbling with; be humble about your gifts and talents, meaning—don't think they are of your own making—they come from God; be merciful to anyone who has offended you.

When you do the simple things any five-year-old could say, you become aware of the Christ light reflected from the depths of your being. Others around you are affected by it, for they are a part of you. Indeed, we are all pieces of a great mirror made up of many holy ones from many traditions, all reflecting the light of Christ, for better or for worse.

So, whether you meditate in a tree or in a pew, remember that it is the light of Christ that makes you shine like those standing around the throne in the Book of Revelation. Their robes were white from being washed in the blood of the Lamb, who is Christ. Like them, we open ourselves to that light.

Questions for Further Discussion:

1. What does it mean to remember your dignity and live a life consistent with that dignity?

2. What does it mean that we come to holiness through the mercy of Christ?

64
A TALE OF TWO PHARISEES
Thirty-first Sunday in Ordinary Time (A)

- Malachi 1:14b–2:2b, 8–10
- 1 Thessalonians 2:7b–9, 13
- Matthew 23:1–12

There are Pharisees and there are Pharisees.

The readings we have just heard might be titled, "A Tale of Two Pharisees." In the Gospel reading, Jesus criticizes the Pharisees and cautions his listeners to do as they *say*, not as they *do*. In the second reading from Thessalonians, however, we hear from another Pharisee, the apostle St. Paul, the great evangelist of the early Church.

What distinguishes these two, the Pharisee of Matthew, chapter 23, and the other Pharisee, St. Paul? Why do the Pharisees in the Gospel come under such constant, sharp criticism from Jesus, while Paul, the other Pharisee, is held in such high esteem?

The difference is the friendship of Christ.

Compare what the readings say about the two Pharisees and then ask yourself which you would want to have as a friend. In Matthew, the Pharisees are described as people who "tie up heavy burdens hard to carry and lay them on people's shoulders, but they will not lift a finger to move them" (23:4). They are self-absorbed, widening their phylacteries and lengthening their tassels. They would take the seats of honor at banquets and synagogues.

Would you want someone like that for a friend?

Now, contrast that description of a Pharisee with the other Pharisee in the second reading, St. Paul. Paul says of his involvement with the Thessalonians, "We were gentle among you, as a nursing mother cares for her children. With such affection for you, we were determined to share with you not only the gospel of God, but our very selves as well, so dearly beloved had you become to us" (1 Thess 2:7–8). Paul says he worked day and night so as not to burden his friends. Now, that's a real friend—someone who will not place extra burdens on you, but will, instead, care for you with the love a mother has for her child. When someone treats us that way, we experience true friendship, we experience Christ.

Christ made the difference in the lives of these two Pharisees. Paul's conversion to Christ on the road to Damascus was a transforming experience of the friendship of Christ. Through his friendship with Christ, Paul was restored to a right relationship with God and other people. He was no longer a prisoner within his own ego. Friendship with Christ drew him out of himself and enabled him to be a Christian friend to those he met. Paul became the model of Christian friendship.

Paul was the bearer of the gospel of Christ, and the bearer of Christian friendship as well. That Paul recognized this connection between the gospel and Christian friendship is clear, for he says in the second reading that he and his companions were determined to share "not only the gospel of God, but our very selves as well." Sharing our very selves is what Christian friendship is all about.

And now comes the good news—by accepting the friendship God offers us in Christ, we too can become true Christian friends in our world. We can break out of the prison that our ego places us in; we can experience again the relationship with others God intends for us.

What an important lesson we can learn from Paul as we seek to be evangelists in the twenty-first century. Paul teaches that if we want to bring people to the good news, if we want to fill the pews with believing, practicing Catholics, we must first become friends with them. We must share not only the gospel of God but our very selves as well. People come to Christ through friendship, because Christ *is* friendship.

When I say, "Christ is friendship," I know this teaching is sound, because I learned it from another deacon. In this case, a deacon of the Church of the fourth century. His name is Evagrius Ponticus, born in 354 at Pontus in Asia Minor, sometimes referred to as Cappadocia, what would be modern-day Turkey.[36] He was ordained a deacon by St. Gregory Nazianzen, and later became archdeacon in the Church. He was regarded as highly gifted and a skilled defender of the faith. However, Evagrius's real journey to the knowledge of Christ as friendship began after he fled his high Church position in the midst of scandal. He went first to a monastery in Jerusalem where he formed a lasting friendship with Melania and Rufinus. Later he would be led to the desert of Egypt where he wrote many beautiful books on the spiritual life. But it is not just his formal works on theology that have enriched our tradition; it is his letters to friends. Evagrius wrote that the spiritual life is a gradual progression of light, leading to the awareness that "grace and friendship liberate." The culmination of the spiritual life for Evagrius was expressed in the simple formula, "Christ is friendship."

Evagrius was a disciple of a controversial theologian of the early Church, a man named Origen. Among other things, Origen said the blood of the Logos (Christ) circulates through scripture. That is why it is a humbling, even terrifying, experience to handle the word of God through proclamation and preaching. But I would go a step further than Origen. I would say that when the word of God is proclaimed well, when it is received in our hearts, then the blood of Christ circulates among us as friendship. The blood of friendship gives us new life, new energy, new commitment to changing our world from a loose association of individuals to a world held together through the bonds of friendship.

The Pharisee of Jesus' time had all the knowledge that the Hebrew scriptures could give him, but without knowing Christ, he was, as Paul would say, "a noisy gong or a clanging cymbal." He had not come to the knowledge of Christ as friendship.

Our desire for knowledge is part of our human nature. If circumstances permitted, many of us would love to spend our time enjoying the luxury of learning, perhaps a masters of divinity. But the important truth this tale of two Pharisees teaches us is that great learning is no substitute for friendship, for Christ is friendship. Perhaps what is needed in our day are not masters of divinity so much as masters of friendship.

Christ is friendship! People come to know Christ through our friendship. It's that simple. It is through our ordinary lives that this truth is proclaimed: Christ is friendship!

Questions for Further Discussion:

1. Does your friendship with Christ enable you to be a better friend to others?

2. What does Evagrius mean when he says, "Grace and friendship liberate"?

65
WHY NOT WAKE UP THIS MORNING?
Thirty-second Sunday in Ordinary Time (A)

- Wisdom 6:11–16
- 1 Thessalonians 4:13–16
- Matthew 25:1–13

We hear in today's Gospel parable a quaint story that, at first reading, may not seem to have much to do with us. But upon deeper reflection, we see that Jesus is describing the very condition of our relationship with God. To reach this understanding, it is helpful to reflect on what preceded this story, the prequel to the parable, if you will.

There was a time, long before this parable was spoken, when our race lived in perfect harmony with God. God was the source of all light and love. It was a time when lamps were not needed, for we lived in the perfect light of God's presence. There was no need of oil then, for we lived by the light of wisdom, resplendent and unfading. It was a time when distinctions were not made between wise and foolish virgins, for we had not yet taken upon ourselves the heavy burden of judging. There was no danger of falling asleep then, and missing the bridegroom, for all were fully awake and alive in the love of God.

But something happened to disturb this experience of being fully awake and aware in the full light of God. Some speak of a fall from grace. The Hebrew scriptures depict a time when Adam and Eve were evicted from paradise, the Garden of Eden. Others speak of a time when humankind became marked with the stain of sin. But we might also speak of what happened as a time when our race fell into a deep sleep, a slumber stretching over eons from which we still struggle to free ourselves.

And yet even as we slept, we never lost our longing for the light. Even today we cherish the faint memory of that full experience of light and love.

And God did not leave us languishing in the slumber of sin. God sent his Son into the world, shouting, "Wake up!"

Wake up! I am the Light of the world that was present to God in the beginning.

Wake up! I am the Light that shines on in the darkness and the darkness will not overcome it.

Wake up! The Kingdom of God is in your midst.

And at the end of today's Gospel: "Stay awake!"

Christ came into the world to wake us up. But what does that mean? What does it mean that Christ wants to wake us up? It has nothing to do with physical sleep, although it helps if we are awake physically. Rather, it has to do with raising our consciousness, of becoming more aware of objective reality.

Christ wakes us up to two great realities. First, when we are fully awake and aware, we become more conscious of the reality of God's love. We have heard many times that God is love, that God loves us unconditionally, that God cannot stop loving us. But so often we hear those words from a somnolent, dreamlike state, where the reality of this tremendous love does not really penetrate into our consciousness. Christ wants to wake us up, to make us conscious, to experience, as we never have before, the reality of love our Creator has for us. Our heightened awareness and experience of this indescribable love we may call contemplation.

At the same time as he is awakening us to the reality of God's love, Christ awakens us to the other great reality: the unity of all creation. In the words of John Donne, "No one is an island." We are all part of the whole. The single mother struggling to survive on welfare is my sister and her suffering is my suffering. The man whose death is reported in the evening news is my brother and his family's anguish is my anguish. The joy of new life when a child is born is my joy. The hope for the future when a couple is joined in the sacrament of matrimony is my hope. Christ awakens us, raises our consciousness to be aware of all this. We call this awareness "compassion."

How then does Christ awaken us? He awakens us through the gentle touch of his word, when we listen attentively to the scriptures, when we feel that faint stirring within us, that soft whisper of truth. He awakens us when we hear the cry of someone in need and we respond in whatever way we are able. He awakens us par excellence when we taste his presence in the body and blood of Christ here at this altar. Christ awakens us so that we may come to the Eucharist with the eyes of our souls wide open and ready to gaze upon the Truth. Christ awakens us so we may experience both contemplation and compassion.

The parable is saying to us, Stay awake to the appearance of Christ in the places of your life where you may not expect him. Stay awake for the coming of Christ in the ordinary events of your day. Be awake to meet Christ when he comes in the disguise of suffering and weakness. Wake up and welcome Christ the way one greets a bridegroom. Wake up, embrace the Bridegroom, fall in love with him.

When we are in love, no one has to tell us to stay awake. Why not fall in love with Christ? Why not wake up and take joy in all that the Bridegroom brings with him?

Perhaps no one has said it better than the Indian poet, Kabir, who in the fifteenth century gave us these marvelous lines:

> Friend, wake up! Why do you go on sleeping?
> The night is over—do you want to lose the day the same way?
> Other women who managed to get up early have
> already found an elephant or a jewel...
> So much was lost already while you slept...
> and that was so unnecessary!
>
> My inside, listen to me, the greatest spirit,
> the teacher is near,
> wake up, wake up!
>
> Run to his feet—
> he is standing close to your head right now.
> You have slept for millions and millions of years.
> Why not wake up this morning?...
>
> Oh, friend, I love you, think this over
> carefully! If you are in love,
> then why are you asleep?[37]

Why not wake up this morning? If you are in love, why are you asleep?

Questions for Further Discussion:

1. What does it mean to you when Christ says at the end of today's Gospel, "Stay awake!"?

2. How has God awakened you at times in your spiritual journey?

66
RISKING IT ALL FOR LOVE
Thirty-third Sunday in Ordinary Time (A)

- Proverbs 31:10–13, 19–20, 30–31
- 1 Thessalonians 5:1–6
- Matthew 25:14–30

If the servants in today's Gospel parable were investment counselors or financial advisors, which would you choose to advise you on investing your life savings? The answer seems obvious. Either of the first two, and certainly not the third. The first two would both be prudent choices; the latter would spell disaster. We have something to learn from each of the servants.

Each of the servants, or financial advisors, if you will, was given something extremely valuable. The first financial wizard receives five talents, the second, two, and the third, only one. The first two seem to have been smart investors. Each doubled his investment and earned the praise of the investor.

The third was not so lucky. He seems to have been in the wrong business. Afraid of taking risks, even with someone else's money, perhaps cautious by nature, he simply put the capital under his mattress and waited for the investor to return. Needless to say, he did not share in his Master's joy.

The beauty of the parables is that they tease us into discovering truth in concrete, ordinary things, not just in abstractions. Most of us know something about the world of investment. We know that it requires careful planning but, also, a certain amount of risk. The connection to the spiritual world is not merely by analogy. The processes inherent in the natural world of making money are intrinsic to the spiritual world as well. We can learn about the life of the spirit by observing how a grain of wheat sprouts and grows; we can also learn from how investors ply their trade.

What then does this parable say to us?

It says, first of all, that we have been given something very precious by someone with an abundance of riches. The choice of the word *talent* is key, for at the time of Jesus it represented something of great value. A talent was something the equivalent of ten years' pay for an ordinary laborer. Our word *talent* comes from that understanding. Thus, we speak of someone who has talent in dancing, or singing, or writing poetry. But by comparison, the talent we are given in the spiritual life has to far exceed any ordinary humanly acquired talent. The talent we are given by God is the capacity to know and love God.

We are given a talent that is unlimited, infinite—the capacity to love God as we are loved by God. And the parable teaches that each is given a different capacity. But each is capable of expanding, stretching, until his or her love reaches its full capacity. Whether the number you place on it is five doubled, or two doubled, or one thousand doubled, the truth revealed by this ordinary aspect of human life is that cooperation with the Divine Investor doubles our money! It is possible to love God to the full capacity God intended for each of us. Whether that capacity is that of a thimble or of a glass, the result is the same—we reach our God-given capacity and share in the Master's joy.

How do we reach our capacity for loving? The answer is suggested by another very ordinary image we came across in the first reading—the worthy wife. If we can get beyond what may first appear as a prefeminist critique of marital relations, we will find hints of how to grow the talent of love we have been given. The answer is simple: We must be worthy wives!

God has entrusted the talent of eternal life to us to be cared for as worthy wives. Our prayer, our silence, our participation in the sacraments become our loving hands, spinning the coarse material of life, turning it into something useful, even beautiful. With hands that touch the poor, with arms that reach out to the needy, we become what God intended us to be—great lovers who share in their Master's joy.

By now it should be clear what this parable is teaching us. But what can we say about the third servant, the one who did nothing to reach his full capacity to love. Why did he not spin? Why did he not reach out to the poor and needy? Why did he not stretch to his full capacity for loving as God intended?

The third servant personifies the fear that stands as the greatest obstacle to our becoming what God intended us to be. There is a place for prudence in the life of the spirit just as there is in the investment world. But we know as well that there are times when we must overcome our fear and take certain risks if we are to grow. Sometimes we must even risk it all. There is risk involved in making a commitment to marriage, the priesthood, the religious life; there is risk involved in having children, in vows of chastity and obedience; there is risk involved in being a young person as much as there is in simply growing old. But with the risk comes greater joy—the Master's joy that is shared in an astronomical return with those who risk loving.

Three servants. Three financial advisors. Each has something to teach us, for the parables of Jesus are always about real human life. They are in a sense alive. They have never stopped growing since the day Jesus first spoke them. To those who heard them directly from Jesus, they probably meant something much different than they did to those who heard them from Matthew, or who first heard them read in a church in Europe or Cappadocia. They are still alive today. And so it is appropriate to ask: What do they say to you? Which servant, which financial advisor, do you choose to imitate? Are you a worthy wife? Are you willing to risk it all so that your love might reach its full capacity?

Questions for Further Discussion:

1. With which of the servants-financial advisors would you invest your talents?

2. Are you willing to take a risk with your talents? In what way?

67
IMAGINE
Feast of Christ the King (A)

- Ezekiel 34:11–12, 15–17
- 1 Corinthians 15:20–26, 28
- Matthew 25:31–46

A few years before he was killed in New York City, John Lennon came out with a song called "Imagine." For those of us who grew up with the Beatles, "Imagine"'s simple melody and lyrics still resonate deeply. It is a song that invites listeners to imagine a different world, a better world. And that is what we are called to do on this feast of Christ the King—imagine a better world.

Here are the lines of the song, "Imagine":

> Imagine there's no countries
> It isn't hard to do
> Nothing to kill or die for
> And no religion too
> Imagine all the people
> Living life in peace

Now, I am sure John Lennon did not have in mind the feast of Christ the King when he wrote these words. But I recite them, because they remind us of something that is badly needed in our Christian world— imagination. Throughout the liturgical year that ends today we have been given all the pieces we need to create a world in which Christ is truly King. What is lacking, what is sadly absent from our Christian world, is imagination.

We use our imagination to create images of the world we live in. A word that is sometimes used to describe the way we conceive of our world is *paradigm*. A paradigm is a model, a pattern, a lens, if you will, through which we view the world around us.

Let me give you some examples. My mother was a remarkably frugal person. She pinched pennies, used things up, stashed money away, just in case there were "hard times." Her paradigm of the world was formed during the Great Depression. Like many others of her generation, she saw the world as a place of scarcity, a place where there might not be enough to go around. And so she saved and scrimped and made do.

The generation that went through World War II formed a different paradigm. They saw the world as a place in which hostile forces could be overcome by the forces of freedom, even if it meant dropping nuclear bombs.

Those of us who came of age during the Vietnam War years also constructed a paradigm that colored the way we saw the world. Many of us who lived during that era are still uncomfortable with talk of war, with unquestioning patriotism, and with politicians who seem eager to start wars. That is the paradigm with which some of us measure the world.

Today, our view of the world is shaped by the events of September 11, 2001. The paradigm for us now includes the World Trade Center towers tumbling down, terrorists with bombs in their shoes, people of a different culture and religion who seem determined to destroy what we hold most dear. The words that best describe our current paradigm are fear, anxiety, and vulnerability. The paradigm of fear affects the way we vote, the civil rights we are willing to give up, and the way we are willing to spend our tax dollars.

But on this Sunday the Church lifts up a paradigm that supersedes all others. All the paradigms I have described are only partial. They are tentative, provisional models for constructing our world. As Catholic Christians, the ultimate paradigm is Christ the King.

We proclaim on this Sunday that the paradigm of Christ, the Shepherd King, describes our world. And what a difference that makes. Imagine living in a world that saw all things through the great lens of Christ the King. Our task today is to imagine. Imagine such a world.

And it isn't hard to do. We start the liturgical year with Advent and Christmas. The incarnation teaches that our God is not a God of scarcity, not a penny-pinching God who stores away goodness and grace. No, our God is a God of great generosity and abundance. We see a God who loved us so much that he had to be among us. And we know that the generosity God has displayed in the past is not exhausted. We need not fear that there will not be enough to go around. In God's household, there is always enough to go around. Can you imagine such a world?

Can you imagine a world in which fear does not control the way we think, the way we live, the way we relate to one another?

Can you imagine a world in which vulnerability is embraced as part of the paschal mystery. How many times during this past year did you hear Christ saying, "Do not be afraid"? Or "Fear is useless"? These are the very same words with which the late John Paul II opened his twenty-six-year pontificate! The events that produce feelings of fear and vulnerability are but further opportunities to trust in God's providence, even if it means the cross.

Can you imagine a world without fear, with nothing to kill or die for? Can you imagine people living in peace? Can you imagine a world in which all religions are one in their source, which is Christ?

Paradigms are formed when people are touched at a deep level by life-changing events. That is true in every age. If we approach our world through the paradigm of 9/11, or some other lesser paradigm, rather than the paradigm of Christ the King, it is because those events have touched us more deeply than Christ has. The task of the Church, our purpose during the entire liturgical year, is to create opportunities for Christ to touch our lives so deeply that a new paradigm is formed—the paradigm of Christ the King.

The song "Imagine" also has these lines:

> You may say I'm a dreamer
> But I'm not the only one
> I hope someday you will join us
> And the world will be as one.

The words I have used to describe the paradigm of Christ the King are the words of a dreamer. Surely, it is naïve to suggest that we imagine a world in which nation-states have been abandoned, where there is no longer anything to kill or die for. Perhaps only a dreamer could speak of a world living in peace. But isn't that the kind of king we are dealing with? A dreamer-king! Christ was the greatest dreamer of all time. And if we are to be his followers, doesn't that commit us to being dreamers as well?

St. Paul speaks of being fools for Christ. Indeed, that is what we are. But therein lies hope for our world: that in every generation there would be some people, perhaps not many, but some, who would dare to imagine a world shaped by the paradigm of Christ.

Can you imagine such a world?

Questions for Further Discussion:

1. What would you add to the paradigm of Christ the King?

2. Can you imagine a world viewed through such a paradigm? How do we create it? Has the liturgical year helped you to create such a paradigm?

NOTES

INTRODUCTION

1. Thomas Merton, *Seeds of Contemplation* (New York: New Directions, 1949), 17.

PART ONE

1. Manfred Weber, ed., *Christmas with Dietrich Bonhoeffer* (Minneapolis: Augsburg Books, 2005).

Homily 1

2. Abraham J. Heschel, *The Prophets*, vol. I (New York: Harper & Row, 1962).

3. Ibid., 4.

4. Ibid., 10.

5. Ibid., 12.

Homily 2

6. John O'Donnel, SJ, *Hans Urs Von Balthasar* (London & New York: Continuum, 1991), 72.

7. Ibid.

Homily 3

8. Alfred Delp, SJ, *The Prison Meditations of Father Alfred Delp* (New York: Herder & Herder, 1963).

9. Ibid., 21.

Homily 4

10. Brendan Doyle, *Meditations with Julian of Norwich* (Santa Fe, NM: Bear & Company, 1983), 48.

11. Alfred Delp, SJ, *The Prison Meditations of Father Alfred Delp* (New York: Herder & Herder, 1963), 34.

12. Ibid., 21.

PART TWO

1. Henri J. M. Nouwen, Donald P. McNeill, and Douglas A. Morrison, *Compassion: A Reflection on the Christian Life* (New York: Image Books, Doubleday, 1983).

Homily 7

2. Gerard Manley Hopkins, "God's Grandeur," in *Gerard Manley Hopkins: A Selection of His Poems and Prose,* ed. W. H. Gardner (Baltimore: Penguin Books, 1953), 27.

Homily 8

3. Raymond E. Brown, SS, *The Birth of the Messiah* (New York: Doubleday, 1977, 1993), 420.

4. Roberto S. Goizueta, "Resurrection at Tepeyac: The Guadalupan Encounter, " *Theology Today* 56 (1999): 336.

Homily 9

5. Joseph Brodsky, "Nativity Poem"(trans. Seamus Heaney) in *Christmas at the New Yorker (The New Yorker Magazine,* Random House, 2003), 289.

6. Raymond E. Brown, SS, *The Gospel According to John,* Anchor Bible Series (I–XII) (Garden City, NY: Doubleday, 1966), 18.

Homily 10

7. Raymond E. Brown, SS, *The Birth of the Messiah* (New York: Doubleday, 1977, 1993), 203.

Homily 11

8. Raymond E. Brown, SS, *Reading the Gospels with the Church: From Christmas Through Easter* (Cincinnati, OH: St. Anthony Messenger Press, 1966), 9.

9. Ibid., 10.

10. Ibid., 89, Appendix, "The Historical Truth of the Gospels"— *Instruction* of the Roman Pontifical Biblical Commission (1964).

11. Ibid., 90.

Homily 12

12. James R. Brockman, *The Violence of Love* (Maryknoll, NY: Orbis Books, 2004).

Homily 13

13. Karl Rahner, SJ, "Towards a Fundamental Theological Interpretation of Vatican II," in *Vatican II: The Unfinished Agenda,* eds. Lucien Richard, OMI, Daniel T. Harrington, SJ, and John W. O'Malley (Mahwah, NJ: Paulist Press, 1987), 14.

PART THREE

1. Archbishop George H. Niederauer, *Precious as Silver: Imagining Your Life with God* (Notre Dame, IN: Ave Maria Press, 2004), 9.

Homily 14

2. *Intermountain Catholic,* January 10, 2003, 12.

3. For an excellent discussion of the controversy surrounding John the Baptist, see Raymond E. Brown, *The Gospel According to John,* Anchor Bible Series (I–XII) (New York: Doubleday & Co., 1970), 41–72.

4. John P. Meier, *A Marginal Jew: Rethinking the Historical Jesus, Volume Two: Mentor, Message, and Miracles* (New York: Doubleday, 1994), 21.

5. Ibid., 19.

Homily 15

6. *The Gift: Poems by Hafiz: The Great Sufi Master,* trans. Daniel Ladinsky (New York: Penguin Compass, 1999), 11.

7. Ibid., 17.

Homily 16

8. *Catechism of the Catholic Church* (New York: William H. Sadlier, Inc., 1994), 1718.

9. *Angelic Spirituality: Medieval Perspectives on the Ways of Angels,* trans. and introduced by Steven Chase (Mahwah/New York: Paulist Press, 2002).

10. Ibid., 25.

11. Ibid., 27–28.

Homily 17

12. Thomas Merton, ed., *Gandhi on Non-Violence* (New York: New Directions, 1964), 26.

13. Ibid., 34.

14. Ibid., 40.

15. Ibid., 65.

PART FOUR

1. *The Confessions of St. Augustine*, trans. Rev. Msgr. John K. Ryan (Garden City, NY: Doubleday, 1960), 254.

Homily 18

2. Sheryl Frances Chen, OCSO, "Why Do We Choose Misery?" *Cistercian Studies Quarterly* 36:3 (2001): 367.

Homily 19

3. I am indebted in this homily to Johannes Baptist Metz, *Poverty of Spirit* (New York: Newman Press, 1968).

Homily 23

4. Thomas Merton, "Toward a Theology of Prayer," *Cistercian Studies Quarterly* 13 (1978): 193.

PART FIVE

1. Dag Hammarskjöld, *Markings* (New York: Alfred A Knopf, 1966), 126.

PART SIX

1. Unpublished poem by Sister Bridget Clare McKeever, SSL.

Homily 31

2. Raymond E. Brown, SS, *The Gospel According to John,* Anchor Bible Series (I–XII) (New York: Doubleday, 1966), 396.

3. Donal Dorr, *Integral Spirituality* (Maryknoll, NY: Orbis Books, 1990), 200.

Homily 33

4. "Day of Prayer Excludes LDS Faith," *Ogden Standard Examiner* (Ogden, UT), May 5, 2004.

5. Ibid.

6. "Offering up Prayer: National Observance Brings Together Weber Pastors, Residents," *Ogden Standard Examiner* (Ogden, UT), May 7, 2004.

Homily 34

7. Jean Leclercq, OSB, "The Mystery of the Ascension in the Sermons of Saint Bernard," *Cistercian Studies Quarterly* 25:1 (1990): 13.

8. Ibid.

9. G. E. H. Palmer, Philip Sherrard, and Kallistos Ware, eds., *The Philokalia*, vol. I (London: Faber & Faber, 1979), 292.

10. Ibid.

Homily 35

11. *The Oxford Dictionary of Literary Quotations,* Peter Kemp, ed. (London: Oxford University Press, 1997), 156.

Homily 36

12. David Schiller, *The Little Zen Companion* (New York: Workman Publishing, 1994), 1.

PART SEVEN

1. Walter M. Abbott, SJ, ed., and Very Rev. Msgr. Joseph Gallagher, trans., ed., *The Documents of Vatican II* (New York: America Press, 1966), 199.

Homily 38

2. Karl Rahner, SJ, *Foundations of Christian Faith: An Introduction to the Idea of Christianity* (New York: Seabrook Publications, 1978), 133.

3. Ibid., 136.

4. Ibid., 136.

Homily 40

5. Abraham J. Heschel, *The Prophets,* vol. 1 (New York: Harper & Row, 1962), 59.

6. Ibid., 57.

7. Ibid., 59.

8. Ibid., 59.

Homily 42

9. Julian of Norwich, *Showings,* Edmund Colledge, OSA, and James Walsh, SJ, eds. (New York: Paulist Press, 1978), 324–25.

Homily 43

10. Jack Kornfield and Christina Feldman, *Soul Food: Stories to Nourish the Spirit & the Heart* (San Francisco: Harper Collins Publishers, 1991), 325.

Homily 44

11. St. John of the Cross, "Prayer of a Soul Taken with Love," in *The Collected Works of St. John of the Cross,* trans. Kieran Kavanaugh, OCD, and Otilio Rodriguez, OCD (Washington, DC: Washington Province of Discalced Carmelites, Inc., 1979), 669.

Homily 46

12. Laura Swan, *The Forgotten Desert Mothers: Sayings, Lives, and Stories of Early Christian Women* (Mahwah, NJ: Paulist Press, 2001).

13. Thomas Merton, *The Wisdom of the Desert* (New York: New Directions, 1960), 40.

Homily 47

14. Brendan Doyle, *Meditations with Julian of Norwich* (Santa Fe, NM: Bear & Company, 1983), 48.

Homily 49

15. T. S. Eliot, "Ash Wednesday," in *Collected Poems* (New York: Harcourt, Brace & World, Inc., 1970), 95.

16. *The Language of Life: A Festival of Poets/Bill Moyers,* James Haba, ed. (includes an interview with poet Joy Harjo) (New York: Doubleday, 1995), 168.

Homily 51

17. Thomas Merton, *Seeds of Contemplation* (New York: New Directions, 1949), 100.

18. Walter M. Abbott, SJ, and Very Rev. Msgr. Gallagher, trans., ed., *The Documents of Vatican II* (New York: The America Press, 1966), 90–91.

Homily 52

19. For this homily, I am indebted to Judith Gundry-Volf, "Spirit, Mercy, and the Other," *Theology Today* 51:4 (1995): 508.

Homily 55

20. *The Anchor Bible Dictionary,* 1st ed., s.v. "Satan."

21. Ibid.

Homily 56

22. Guy Gaucher, *The Story of a Life: St. Thérèse of Lisieux* (New York: HarperCollins, 1993), 122.

23. Ibid., 123.

24. Robert N. Bellah, et. al., *Habits of the Heart: Individualism and Commitment in American Life* (New York: Harper & Row, 1986).

Homily 58

25. Jessica Powers, "The Mercy of God," in *The Selected Poetry of Jessica Powers* (Washinton, DC: ICS Publications 1999), 1.

Homily 61

26. Antoine de Saint-Exupéry, *The Little Prince,* trans. Katherine Woods (New York: Harcourt Brace Jovanovich, 1943).

27. Ibid., 70.

Homily 62

28. Thomas Bullfinch, *Bullfinch's Mythology: The Age of Fable* (Garden City, NY: Doubleday, 1968), 162.

29. Ibid., 163–64.

30. Annie Dillard, "Schedules," in *The Best American Essays 1989,* ed. Geoffrey Wolff (New York: Ticknor & Fields, 1989), 72.

Homily 63

31. *Summum v. City of Ogden,* No. 01-4022 (10th Cir. July 19, 2002).

32. Martin Buber, *Tales of the Hasidim: Early Masters* (New York: Schocken Books, 1947, 1975), 149.

33. *Love: A Fruit Always in Season: Daily Meditations from the Words of Mother Teresa of Calcutta,* Dorothy S. Hunt, ed. (San Francisco: Ignatius Press, 1987), vii.

Homily 64

34. Stephen Mitchell, "Notes on the Tao Te Ching," *Living Prayer* 23:6 (Nov.–Dec. 1990): 19.

35. Thomas Merton, *Mystics and Zen Masters* (New York: Noonday Press, 1967), 20.

Homily 65

36. Abbot John Eudes Bamberger, OCSO, "Desert Calm—Evagrius Ponticus: The Theologian as Spiritual Guide," *Cistercian Studies Quarterly* 27.3 (1992): 185.

Homily 66

37. Robert Bly, ed., *The Kabir Book: Forty-four of the Ecstatic Poems of Kabir* (Boston: Beacon Press, 1977), 3, 13, 41.